Gifted Momma and Her Guides

A book based on my own personal experiences of how I adapted to my intuition to feel comfortable in my own mind, body, and soul as a psychic medium.

Included are the true stories of local cold cases of Tolland County, Connecticut!

Susan Sapolis Mahon

Hearing from Heaven, LLC.

Library of Congress Cataloging-in-Publication Data
Name: Mahon, Susan Sapolis, author.
Title: Gifted Momma and Her Guides / Susan Sapolis Mahon.
Identifiers: ISBN 979-8-218-37078-7
Subjects: 1. BODY, MIND & SPIRIT / Angels & Spirit Guides
2. BODY, MIND & SPIRIT / Channeling & Mediumship. 3.
BODY, MIND & SPIRIT / Parapsychology / ESP (Clairvoyance,
Precognition, Telepathy).

Photographs © Susan Sapolis Mahon

DONATION INFORMATION

20% of the proceeds from the sale of this book will be donated to the American Foundation for Suicide Prevention of Connecticut in memory of Jim and Steve, under their real names.

This book is dedicated to 3 *amazing* souls:
Jim and Steve (*my spirit guides*),
and my Sweetpea, who also loved chasing butterflies.

These are Jim and Steve's handprints:

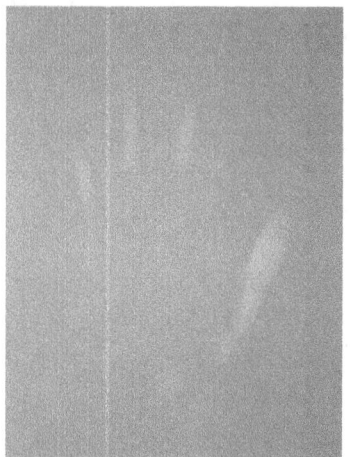 

This image shows Sweetpea's head, shoulders, and chest.

This image matches a family photo of hers.

As I wrote this book, I used my own personal experiences that I have endured through this journey that stemmed from my childhood memories and my past lives to how I met my guides, Steve and Jim, along with Sweetpea.

I am very excited to share my story along with Steve, Jim's, and Sweetpea's, as they chose me to be their anchor and voice on this earth, to finally have their stories heard and listened to.

Many thanks to my parents in heaven,
with their *massive* support and direction as I take this
journey.

NOTE TO THE READER

The names of the individuals mentioned in this book have been changed. However, the names of the towns and places mentioned are all the real places where these incidents took place. The police have the hardcopy of this book with the real names. My goal for this book is to bring forth the truth that Tolland County, Connecticut has needed for many decades.

Table of Contents

INTRODUCTION

She was a girl chasing butterflies. She was a girl chasing rainbows. She was a girl chasing her dreams, if only she knew what they were. She was a girl who couldn't understand the things around her. She would ask about these things and would receive no answers. She would let anyone get close to her as she was hoping to seek those answers.

She would remember things that never happened. She would feel the pain of losing someone she never met. She would remember in detail places she had never been to. She would miss a place she never knew existed. She couldn't understand her own thoughts, feelings, or emotions, and how they all tied together.

She didn't fit in and she knew she was different from others; her own family, siblings, and friends never understood her completely. She would accept the defeat and the pain that would go with it. She would describe the things she saw, heard, and knew, but couldn't explain how she knew such information. She looked to the past and remembered what was. She adored the past and how it was portrayed to her in such a clear way, like she knew the places and they felt familiar to her.

She was a shy, sweet, innocent child. She loved and adored all who were around her despite the laughing, jokes, and comments that were made about her and to her. She was always there for others rather than putting herself first, even though it was tiring and ran her down. She endured a lot of emotional pain and low self-esteem and lack of confidence due to others making fun of her and making her question her own mentality. She went along with it, as it was easier, but she knew something wasn't right.

She felt alone, as if no one understood her. She would remain the lone wolf well into her adult life. As she didn't know what her purpose was. She prayed for the answers as much as she could until one day, as a young woman, she knew the answers were within.

She sought, she listened, and she understood everything she needed to know when her guides came to her, literally face-to-face and heart-to-heart, and taught her the rest of the way to who she is meant to be and who she is today with their unconditional love, support, patience, laughter, and silly antics that made her laugh, along with the way that they surrounded, escorted, and protected her. She is now a daughter, a sister, an aunt, a mother, a wife, a psychic, a medium, and a remote healer.

That girl is me, **Susan Sapolis Mahon**. As I have grown spiritually, I have listened, learned, and seen a lot of amazing things. My goal is to help others know that it is okay to be in their own mind, body, and soul with their intuitive gifts, that nothing is impossible, and how to accept that our own personal journey can be the most exciting treasure we can ever have, and that every step of that journey will always help someone else in one way or another.

CHAPTER 1

MY EARLY YEARS

In the evening of August 6, 1968, I was born to the most amazing parents on this earth. I was the third child of three. Being the youngest in the family, I found that I saw a lot going on and how different each sibling was from one another. Even though you live in the same house, with the same parents, things aren't always what they seem to be.

My parents loved each other from a very young age and built a life together that lasted many decades. They loved their children unconditionally and were able to give us everything we needed and more as they were a hard-working couple. Dad worked from sunup to sundown building houses, in the hot sun, rain, and even in frigid weather.

Mom was a stay-at-home-mom until I was about nine years old, then she went back to work as a loan officer at a credit union. They always made sure we had everything we needed, along with many extras that came from their heart.

We were a typical, normal family living in the town of Windsor, Connecticut. Dad and Mom both grew up here and decided to raise their family in the same town. Dad built us a house after I was born, and we moved in as a happy family of five. Everything seemed normal as I grew up, yet things felt and looked different to me.

I didn't feel like I fit in anywhere. No one understood me. I was belittled, made fun of by others, even by my siblings, which all led me to have low self-esteem and a lack of confidence. I ended up being a timid child, afraid to speak to others and go after the dreams I would think I would want in life.

As I grew, I noticed the connection I had with my dad. I would hear him tell others that I was his favorite. I would hear this a lot, and I always felt that. I felt and knew after I heard this many times that he understood me, but he couldn't explain why I was the way I was, either. When he talked, I listened and heard what he was saying, and it always stayed with me. He was my rock.

This odd feeling of being out of place grew and grew and got more intense, and it was hard to describe how it felt. I would try to explain it to people and they would laugh at me when I told them things I was experiencing. I was brushed off many times up until my adulthood. I continued to be belittled, made fun of, and called names throughout my childhood and adolescence as people projected their feelings onto me as well. I would believe these things, but at the same time it didn't feel right.

It was easier to ignore it instead of dealing with it, since I didn't know how and obviously no one else did either. I began to brush it all off until things really started to get rolling with many unexplainable instances that I couldn't ignore any longer.

One day, I started to experience many things, and they started to snowball fast. I would hear things clearly, as if they were conversations others were having, but no one was around me. I would see things and people, and then they would be gone. I would feel things and know things before they would happen but couldn't explain why when they did happen. I just knew. I remember this started at the age of 5. The reason that it started at the age of 5 is something which I will go into more in later chapters.

I started to see things fully and live, and then they would be gone. This would happen at night when I was home alone, while I was waiting for my parents to come home. I would hear the car in the driveway and the garage door open so they could pull in. I would look out the window and see them in the car, with Mom waving to me as they pulled into the garage. I was like, "Oh good, now I can go to bed," as I was now nine years old and didn't want to go to sleep alone in the house. I waited and waited, and waited, but they never pulled into the garage. I looked outside the window again, and they were not there. The garage door was not open, and the car was not in the garage or the driveway. They were not home yet! I couldn't understand what had happened. This was the vision I started receiving to let me know they were on their way. They arrived home about thirty minutes later.

Another example of this came when I started to ask my mom if we could go to certain places that I really liked and enjoyed. I would ask to go back to the Lincoln Memorial, and mom would say, "You've never been there!" yet I could describe it in detail.

I would ask many questions, like "Why do I see this, and you don't?" These things started to happen more and more as I grew up.

I had many fears as well, and again, I couldn't understand why I had these fears. I have always hated to be locked in, locked up, or confined. I never lock anything. I even refuse to have a twist tie on bread as I feel trapped, restricted, and confined.

I was afraid of water to a certain point, but not pools. It was water I couldn't see through to the bottom such as lakes, oceans, rivers, and ponds that scared me. I still went in them, but I was not comfortable doing so. I loved pools; we had one growing up and I spent my childhood swimming. I didn't like going underwater, as I would feel freaked out and get breathless, beyond the normal feelings of going under water... and I would see young girls drowning. Again, I would ask about these things, but couldn't get any answers. I wasn't being ignored. It was just that no one had any answers at that time.

As I grew into my teenage years, which is awkward enough for anyone, things started to escalate with overwhelming feelings and fears. I started to notice things more and more, such as I was unable to handle being in small, confined places like the back seats of two-door cars or the far back area in station wagons, yet I could handle being in a closet if I could see an opening. I started to fear large crowds like concerts, fairs, parties, and get-togethers of all kinds as I felt way too overwhelmed, to the point that my ears would block up. It was hard to hear people speak or even hear my own voice, which caused me to not want to speak at all. Plus, everything I looked at was blurry.

Again, I didn't have the answers as to why these things had started to happen and continued to happen. I brushed it off and ignored it, because you know that if you don't address the issue, it's not there, right? I found that I was limiting myself from doing things with my friends because I felt like I had to stick close to home, as it was my comfort zone. I also found myself delegating things to others so I wouldn't have to do them or make up excuses as to why I couldn't do them. It's not that I didn't want to do those things – it was because I felt I couldn't enjoy them with the feelings I was having.

After a while, I stopped asking why these things were happening and gave in to the sensations and lived this way – for the time being.

The one great thing about this was that I got to spend a lot of time with my parents, and with their friends as well. This was something that I didn't mind, as I enjoyed every minute I had with my parents. During this time, I noticed I still wasn't a big talker, but more of a giggler. People loved to see me giggle at them. I hated it, as it got on my own nerves. I couldn't hold a conversation with anyone for too long, though, because overwhelming feelings came about and intervened.

When I was in school it was very, very difficult to focus and learn what I needed to learn, as I felt I could not ask questions or speak in front of people due to being belittled and made fun of. This resulted in having my self-esteem and confidence stolen from me by others who projected their feelings onto me, but again, I did what I could and kept moving forward as I was.

As a teenager, I had a great group of friends. We did a lot together and went through a lot together as well. This group of girls will always be special to me and in my heart. They will never be forgotten.

At the age of 16, I started my first job at a local pizza restaurant. I was so excited to go to work part time, to learn to be independent, and to earn my own money to buy my first car. Then I realized that when I went to work, I would have to speak. This made me extremely nervous, because my voice wouldn't get loud, and if I tried, it was worse – my voice got *high and squeaky*. I couldn't even stand to hear myself talk. It took a long while to outgrow that, but I did.

However, I worked with a great group of people, and it was like having a whole new family. I started to get my self-esteem and confidence back. I will always be grateful for my first job, which I still hold close to my heart to this day for all the lessons I learned there, and I can tell you there were *many*. I always say that time in my life was a massive milestone and full of life-altering changes that I will remember forever. I used those moments to move forward as I continued on my path.

As I grew into my early adult years, I was still very aware of all the feelings and sensations I was experiencing. They continued to intensify to the point that I started to have anxiety and anxiety attacks. With all those feelings coming at me at once, it became way too much for me, but I still moved along. I again started to see people that others didn't and to hear them more often and more clearly. It was like hearing people on a baby monitor, static and all.

I became very interested in the past, particularly to understand what life used to be like back in the day. I was obsessed with pictures, items, towns, and the way people lived and did things to survive back then. I loved learning about old homes and old towns, the Depression Era, the Civil War and World Wars, life during the 1800s, and more. It was like I was missing something I never had or had been to.

I was very interested in bones, bodies, and death, cemeteries, the afterlife, and mysteries. I wanted to learn all about them. I wanted to become an archaeologist, but never believed in myself enough to do that. I was also very interested in ghosts, bones, and dead bodies. I didn't completely understand why I would be so interested in these things, as I didn't understand their history. The passion that I had for these things stayed with me for many, many years to come.

There was a time that I wanted to own and open my own bed and breakfast in New Hampshire in an old house so that I could keep its history alive. I started to take community college classes to learn how I could go about putting my dream into action. It went very slowly, as focusing on learning was difficult and the sensations were still intense. The classes got harder, and the large groups of people were getting to me. I had to stop taking classes and choose another career that I felt would be easier for me and that I could cope with while living with these weird, odd feelings and unexplainable happenings.

Next, I started a full-time job as a customer support representative at a membership wholesale club in town that I loved, and I thought, *well, this will work for me for a long while*, and it did. I grew a lot there as well.

After five years, I was offered another full-time job in town as a telephone operator in a national customer support center for copy machines. As the anxiety and the weird sensations continued, I started to feel lost again and didn't know where to turn, other than to work both jobs and avoid everything else.

Around this time, I moved out on my own for the first time, which was a great thing as I felt in control of my own life and not that my life was in control of me. My roommate and I had a blast, as we had known each other since preschool at the age of three. We lived together and worked both jobs together and had nothing but laughs. This kept me moving along to the next adventure. I started to handle my anxiety differently as I learned more about it and how it worked and what caused it.

I found that anxiety can be a good thing and very helpful, but you need to make it work for you rather than against you. As I did that, things started to change in a good way, and my self-esteem and self-confidence started to increase – not a lot, but it was going in the right direction.

But what also increased were the weird, unexplainable things and sensations, and the knowing of things that would happen... and then happened shortly after I knew they were going to happen. Again, I had to keep moving forward with these unexplainable happenings.

Marriage, Children, and Family

In my late twenties, I met and married the man of my dreams. At this time, I was working full time as a teller in a bank, until I was laid off. I really enjoyed working there, as there were only five of us, so it was not overwhelming at all. After I was laid off, I accepted a job offer at a credit union. I loved working there as well, because my mom was a loan officer there, so we got to share more time together.

I stayed at the credit union until my husband, and I decided to start a family. We had two children. They were and are my everything, my world, my rocks. I stopped working full time in March of 2001 to become a stay-at-home mom for our two children. I did this for twenty-plus years.

That was the hardest but most rewarding job I have ever had, and without regrets. I got to see all their firsts and watch them grow and learn. It wasn't easy, but the things in life that are worth the most are the ones that are not the easiest. When the kids were in school full time, I noticed the sensations increasing again, and at a faster pace.

I had always admired psychics, so I decided to inquire about them and learn everything I could. As I did, things started to make sense, and the pieces fit perfectly into the puzzle, answering the questions I'd had all these years. It was much clearer to me – like a crystal ball.

I continued to raise my family and started to explore and follow my instincts more. I was still fighting the anxiety and anxiety attacks, but I continued to learn more about that as well. I found that they are tied together.

After years of hard work and educating myself, I was getting more and more excited as I learned about psychics and mediums. A psychic is someone that can see the past, present and future. A medium is someone that can connect and communicate with spirits such as a loved one who has passed to bring forth messages to others for peace and direction. Not all psychics are mediums, but I was blessed with both to help others navigate and understand their own personal journeys.

I started my own business, called Hearing from Heaven, and started to offer free practice online chat readings. As I did this, I found that my readings were spot-on. I was amazed and blown away by the information I gave to my clients in my readings that turned out to be so true.

As I continued to raise our family, I became more and more interested in what I was doing as a psychic medium. I knew this was what I was supposed to do, that this was my purpose. My mission is to bring forth messages to others from the Lord, from loved ones who have passed on, and from the universe, along with peace, guidance, and direction in a calming and delicate manner, all without judgment.

The most important things to me were and are my family. We have had our trying times, good times, and excellent, fantastic times as we still do. We get through things together as a team and as a family. Are we perfect? No. But we do belong together and will remain together forever. Our children grew to be wonderful, beautiful adults, fulfilling their dreams and going after what they needed to achieve their purposes on this earth. I could not be any prouder as we were blessed with two amazing children.

Meanwhile, I was learning more about myself and finding it interesting to understand how everything fits together. Life is certainly a puzzle, and it has a path. As I started to educate myself more, my self-esteem and confidence started to grow again. The weird sensations also grew, but the anxiety did not.

I noticed a pattern. I was being drawn to certain things. I was nudged to take pictures and videos, and to look at the sky. I was very drawn to the sky, because it felt like more answers would jump out at me when I focused on it, and in a way, they did. As I did this, I would hear, see, and know more. I was amazed at how I was feeling and what I was seeing. I would gather my pictures and videos and review them repeatedly, and the things I would see and hear were and are remarkable. I kept at this for a long while, and I still go back to this as I'm told to for many reasons, particularly as this is one of my connections to the other side, to spirits and to the universe.

While I was doing my practice readings, I had to start somewhere, right? I met some amazing people, and there was one special person that I call *my sister*. She has stood by me as I have learned about my intuition over all these years. We speak daily to this day. We learn from each other, we understand each other, and we comfort each other, all *without* judgment. We are both psychics and mediums, but our styles are very different. We often combine our intuition together in a reading, if need be, to help a client get the peace and answers they are seeking.

She is my soul sister, my rock, my go-to when I get stuck. We are there for each other through thick and thin. Even though we are a few states apart from one another we remain close, I am happy and proud to call her one of my soulmates. I will always cherish you, my Stevie.

I have continued to learn about myself and my intuition, and I realized this is just for me. *ME*, not the daughter, the aunt, the sister, the mother, the wife, or the friend, but for *ME*.

I finally found the answers and myself and my life's purpose. I will continue this life as I enjoy helping others find the peace, clarity, comfort, direction, and answers they long for in order to help them move forward and accomplish what each person is here to accomplish.

Teamwork is necessary and what this world is lacking, along with compassion, kindness, love, peace, hope, and belief. We need to work together, give more, and forgive one another as we travel on this earth together to make this puzzle complete.

CHAPTER 2

DISCOVERING AND UNDERSTANDING MY ABILITIES

As I mentioned in Chapter 1, we all must work together to make this world go around, and working as a team is the only way to make this happen. I knew that by putting my gifts in order and learning how to use them I could do this to help others do the same - not just other psychics and mediums, but my clients as well. As I continued to learn and understand myself, things started to make sense. I started to get excited and almost overwhelmed with what I needed to learn and understand and put into action.

In this chapter, I will share what abilities I was given with some examples as to how I knew I had them. Each psychic or medium has their own experiences and style, just as doctors have their specialties. I need to have the right connection for the relationship to form and to stay bonded. I have learned and realized with my gifts that living life is not a hard thing to do. If you think about it the basics are all you need, and the rest will fall into place.

It took me a long time to understand everything that was happening. It was a very, very interesting ride. Once I learned everything and understood why all this was happening, I accepted it. I did not ignore any of it, even though what I see, hear, feel, and know is not all pretty and happy.

As with anything in life, there is the good and the bad. This is no different. It's not always good news, happy news, and what you want to hear. It's information straight from your guides, my guides, spirit, the Lord, and the universe, and your loved ones that are giving the messages. I am just the messenger that delivers the information in a kind, compassionate, proper, and loving way. I take my job very seriously, as it is who I am and why I am here.

LIST OF MY ABILITIES

Astral Travel

This is the ability to will your consciousness out of your body and visit places to acquire information and bring it back to the physical realm. Astral travel is known as the soul leaving the body while alive and going to another place. Astral projection can occur in both sleeping and in the waking state.

The example I'm going to use for this is the one when my soul did leave my body and went to England to visit the royal family. The next day, I found myself asking people why the pregnancy of Kate, Prince William's wife, was not being discussed anywhere. It was not on television, in the papers, or on magazine covers.

I would tell people she was having a baby boy, and they would say *"What are you talking about?"* This news of her first pregnancy came out for the world to know one year later, but my soul had traveled there one year earlier, received the news, and brought it back with me. I had traveled out of the country and to the future to get information to bring to the present.

Psychic Typing

This is the ability to have loved ones who have passed on, as well as Lord Jesus and Archangel Michael, type personal messages through me (by online chat readings). Others can also type with me, but in my journey, I work with the Lord and Archangel Michael daily. I also do this with Jim and Steve as an alternative to psychic writing, which I will discuss next.

I came to notice this ability during a reading with a client. It was amazing, as I was told to tell the client to allow the spirit to type with her hands and... boom! The messages came in from all over the place and in detail. I would chime in as well, because they can type through me too.

Some people are not able to do the typing if they are too stressed or nervous. You need to be calm and uninterrupted to do this with me and a spirit. This is my favorite of all. The messages that come through are more than amazing – and they are more meaningful and personal to the client.

Psychic Writing

This I do with my guides and my loved ones who have passed over to receive personal messages through handwritten communication.

I have many notebooks with personal messages from my boys (my guides – Jim and Steve), my parents, my godmother, and other souls I have helped. This is truly amazing, as Steve uses my left hand and Jim uses my right hand.

Dad and Mom and Nana all use my right hand, and my Godmother uses my left, because she was a lefty. She even puts my arm and hand in a lefty setup. I write with my team as much as I can, as I treasure the quiet time and spending time with them in a different way. The hard part is trying to get them to write smaller on the paper, but that's okay, as they are driving the ship.

There have been times when Jim and Steve fought over the pen, and my hands go back and forth as they both want to write at the same time and give me information on certain situations. My pen has literally flown across the room, and I never laughed so hard. They really keep me on my toes.

One time, Steve was writing, and he couldn't make what he was saying clear enough, so he darkened the words repeatedly to get his point across.

I truly enjoy all the messages and information I receive from anyone that writes with me, even though they are not always pleasant messages.

Clairaudience

This is the ability to hear spirits speak, whether it is out loud or in my mind.

It's cool hearing a conversation going on when no one is near or around you.

One night, I was sleeping and was awakened to spirits talking in a group amongst themselves, I had to set a boundary as I needed to sleep. But again, I don't mind, this stuff is just so cool. I really, really love it when it's quiet and suddenly, I hear, *"SUSAN!"* I am like, *"WHAT!?"* and yet there is no one around. It is so amazing to hear voices from heaven.

Clairvoyance

This is the ability to see spirits. I have seen full figures, partial figures, and sometimes just faces and hands. It takes a lot of energy for spirits to show themselves in full figure. However, if they want to show themselves, it is totally up to them.

Here is one example. I love mowing lawns and creating gardens. It was my happy place as a stay-at-home mom. It was something I created and loved with all my heart.

One day in the spring of 2015, I was mowing the yard and felt a heaviness trailing behind me. I felt it the whole time I was mowing. After my work was done, I sat to take a break and, suddenly, I saw my dad, who had passed away in March of that year, walk onto the driveway from the road.

I stood up and started to walk to the end of the driveway, and I saw him wave. He said, *"You did everything right."* He was referring to the fact that I was the one who made the decisions for him at the time of his death. He turned around and faded off into the air.

I also see Steve, a very handsome guy I must say, who appears to me as he was when he was young and in high school in the 1970s. It's such a joy seeing him.

Jim shows me himself in a totally different way. He uses a look-alike and sends them to earth to represent him to let me know he is near and watching over me. The look-alike he sends looks just like him, including the way he dressed and how he walked, down to the bandana he wore around his head with his lovely, soft, flowing, long hair from the 1970s. It is totally amazing and uncanny what spirits can do.

Another example I want to share is lost spirits, earth-bound spirits, which are people that have died and haven't gone into the light yet or don't know they have passed.

One summer, I was working outside, doing online chat readings, when suddenly, I saw a World War II soldier standing to my left about six feet away. He was clearly in uniform, and he wanted to tell me his story.

I started to take notes as I don't really understand military talk and I'm not knowledgeable in WWII history but have always been drawn to it. He told me about how he was shot down in a plane, and I saw that his left arm was clearly damaged.

I reassured him that everything was going to be okay and asked him if he knew if he had been killed. He said yes, but he was lost. I asked him to look for the bright light. I said it was okay to go into it. He started to walk into the light, then turned around and thanked me and waved. I said, "You are very welcome," and I thanked him for his service.

It was such a very calm yet overwhelming experience, and I knew there were going to be more lost souls needing direction, and that I would be there to help. I started to Google the information he had given me; he had shared the name of the plane and rank he was at the time of his death. I found out who he was. He was a fighter pilot in WWII. I was speechless.

Clairsentience

This is the ability to sense and/or feel the energy around you.

My example of this is that when I visit different places, I can feel the energy of others. This happens whether it is good energy or bad energy. I start to feel dizzy. My ears can get blocked up and pop, and my eyes go blurry. I will even get the sensations of being ill from nausea to vomiting to almost passing out. It gets so bad that I must take a break or just move right through it. It's not all bad for me when this comes on. When my mom visits me while sleeping, she will put a blanket on me. Her energy can be so strong that the electricity in her energy is so electrifying. It feels so cool and tingly and fast. I know it's her by the extreme energy connection and bring such comfort to me.

Clairgustance

This is the ability to taste.

This one is interesting. I know when a spirit is trying to communicate with me and get my attention when they sometimes put a flavor of food and/or drink in my mouth that I am not eating or drinking.

My example for this is that one day I was walking along with a friend and, suddenly, I had the taste of maple syrup. I knew right away this was for my friend, and that a spirit wanted me to relay a message to her.

At times, my guides will put the taste of beer in my mouth when they are drinking beer, and say, "CHEERS!" I'm like, "Okay wise guys, you know I don't drink," and they continue to enjoy what they are doing. It's all good.

Claircognizance

This is the ability of knowing.

This was one of the first gifts to develop for me. The ability to know something is *not* always a good thing. Most of the time, it starts with the negative things that will happen, then turns to the good things, which is when a sense of balance comes.

For this, I have a sad example. It was a feeling of knowing something bad was going to happen, and as the time grew closer that feeling intensified. I felt that someone was going to pass away by an unfortunate accident. I felt it was tied to a certain person I knew, so

I talked with that person, and they didn't know or feel anything about this. This went on for about a month and a half. Then one day I got a massive message that it was going to happen soon, like in four days. Four days later, this person I spoke with called and reported exactly what I told them would happen, and it was the most devastating day in their life as it was a young child who had passed.

Another time I felt someone was going to pass, a man, and that it was linked to me, but more on the outskirts or branched off me. A month later, I found out that my first boss, from the job I had when I was 16, had passed away. That hit me like a brick. I realized that this was part of what I was meant to do.

I have a client that I was told to tell her that she should not drive her car on a day trip she was going to be taking soon. I mentioned to her that there was an issue with the fuel pump. She was a bit shocked that I had mentioned that, but she had her husband check it and indeed they found that the fuel pump was damaged and clogged. She emailed me to thank me for the heads up and was able to take another car on their trip.

Claircognition

This is the ability to predict the future.

This one can be fun at times, as I chat with clients in online readings.

It's cool being able to tell them what is coming up for them, whether it's a windfall of money, a new love interest, or a new job.

The best part is when they come back to me or leave a review telling me I was spot on and to thank me for the heads up.

On the flip side, I also get the bad news, like if an accident is going to happen or something will be going wrong, or someone is going to wreak havoc in their lives.

Again, it's not very pleasant, but all part of my job.

Clairalience

This is the ability to smell.

This ability can be cool as well.

Since he passed away, I often get the smell of my dad. I would smell his Chapstick for a very long time. That brought me comfort when he first passed, and it let me know that he was okay.

When my mom passed, I would smell the perfume that I found while cleaning out her house. She knew I loved it, so she would bring forth that smell to let me know she was near, and that she was okay.

Empathy

This is the ability to feel or sense another person's emotions.

This is a very emotional one. If you are someone with a lot of empathy and compassion, you tend to pick up other people's emotions. Whether it's happiness, depression, anger, physical pain, or mental pain, you will get it. At this point you must decipher what is yours and what are other people's emotions.

One experience I had was when I was in a store, just looking around, and a lady came near me. I noticed that I became worried and sad and started to cry. She asked if I was okay. I answered, "Yes, but I don't feel you are." She said, "I'm not. My mother passed away about a week ago." I said, "Yes, I know, she is here with you now and has a message for you." I passed on the message, and she was so grateful and gave me a hug and thanked me. The feelings I was having were hers. It can be very emotional and exhausting going through this, but it is well worth the smile on someone's face as I help them move along in their life. This can be very hard until you are very familiar with doing this.

Mediumship

This is the ability to connect with spirits from the past, who can be relatives or other unrelated spirits.

This is my favorite of all of them. I love taking the time to listen and talk with spirits as they tell their stories and I get to forward messages for them.

I have connected with some amazing souls, even famous spirits like Michael Jackson, Eddie Van Halen,

Steven Clark, and Jimi Hendrix, to name a few. I also connect with missing people that would like to tell me their story.

I love the fact that the musicians come through in readings to help others succeed at their dreams and goals in music as well as they did.

Remote Healing

This is the ability to help heal pain and discomfort, anxiety, PMS, aches, pains, and more.

I do this online in my chat readings. It's truly amazing.

An example is that while I was in a chat reading, I was able to lower a client's heart rate back to normal, as she was having a panic attack at the time.

I do this with my healing hands through the connection I have with the universe as my hands heat up, burn, and tingle. That's my clue to help the client. I will set up my hands and send the energy that I need to and give the client the relief they need at that time.

MY SPECIALTIES

Breakups and Divorce
Destiny and Life Path
Career and Work
Money and Prosperity
General Readings

Family Guidance
Love and Relationships
Deceased Loved Ones
Past Life Readings
Tarot Cards

With all these tools in my spiritual toolbox, I am happy and proud to say I can help bring peace, comfort, guidance, direction, and happiness to others in this world.

CHAPTER 3

MY PAST LIVES AS THEY WERE SHOWN TO ME

I have always been intrigued by past lives and have found them to be very informative. They are stepping-stones that carry you into each life you live. They are packed full of lessons and adventures that we can bring with us to the next life. Sometimes, you don't have a choice, and those lessons will follow you until you have learned and accepted them.

We all have had many lives and experienced many things. Some of them are the same, and some are different, as we are all unique individuals. As a psychic, medium, and remote healer, I am even more intrigued by them, as they are a part of who I am and what I do, and they have brought me to where I am today.

I want to share some of my past lives with you as they were shown and told to me and as I remember them. I will also tell you more about my guides, Jim and Steve, as they are a very *huge* part of *all* my life.

Another reason why I want to share these lifetimes with you is so you can get a feel of where I have been and where I am going with this later in my story.

The Appalachian Indian Chief

One person I remember meeting in a past life from my early childhood is that of an Appalachian Indian Chief. I am not positive of the year, but I can clearly see I met him. He was a very tall man, and he had long, dark, soft, hair with some waves to it. He wore a large and long headdress with many colors and feathers, beads, and ribbon-like material. He was dressed in pants and a coat. I was brought there to meet him and talk to him.

I couldn't see who I was with when we were introduced to each other, but it always felt like I was with my mother – not the mother from the life I am living now. I was a four-year-old white boy with very blond hair that grew past my shoulders. I was dressed in short pants that went to my knees, and they looked light blue. I was barefoot and bare-chested as I had been playing in the running river along the banks of the northeast mountains.

The beautiful Indian chief was large, yet gentle with me. He took my right hand and led me to a wooden structure on the top of the banks. We walked up three steps to the porch. Everything was made of wood of a light-to-medium color, with round poles to hold the ceiling up on the porch. The chief asked me to sit down, and we sat together and talked.

Around us were many teepees and Indian families going about their business. The children were running around having fun, some even getting into mischief. The women were hanging clothes, food was being prepared, and everything that needed to be tended to was being tended to.

As I watched this vision, the chief was talking to me the boy, explaining what was being done. I was taking it all in even though I was only four years old. I understood and felt all the compassion, love, and commitment that these people had for each other. They protected one another. They all had jobs to do and they did them without complaining, only pride.

I looked at the chief, and noticed he had tears running from his eyes. He was very, very proud of his tribe and everything they believed in and stood for. He held my hand out, laid a large red feather in it, and said to me, "Always do your best and help others in need, and never try to be the one to outdo others. It takes a team and teamwork to get what we need accomplished. No one is above anyone else. We are all the same. We may look different, but deep down inside we are the same. It's just how you use the tools to accomplish those goals."

This is why I am so against the holiday of Thanksgiving. I do not feel the need to celebrate the massacre of Indian tribes, as they are very dear and close to my heart.

The Rock Star

It was in the early 1800s – 1812, to be exact. I was traveling barefoot across the hard, cold, dusty land. I was born in Ireland and traveled along the roads and fields with my best friend in the world. We met at an early age and stayed best friends until our deaths. We both had a passion for music. We were able to get a band together, as we both loved to play the guitar.

I loved to write poetry, and my buddy was the one to put it all together to make the poetry into a song. That was his talent then, and in this life too. We traveled the cliffsides with our guitars on our backs as we made our dreams come true.

We met a lot of very interesting people on the way. We also endured many obstacles that would delay our dreams from coming to fruition. We did accomplish it, though. The lesson here again is teamwork. No one was trying to outdo the other. We did it together and enjoyed the journey as we traveled together with our mates.

The most interesting part of this past life is that my buddy lived in this lifetime with me as well. Steve (another Steve) and I did not know each other, but our souls knew each other. He was eight years older than me and lived in the United Kingdom. He had a challenging life, but he accomplished what he wanted. He again had a passion for music and guitars.

He was a musical genius who didn't need to work very hard; his work flowed out of him naturally, and his talent just came through for the world to hear. This young man made his dreams come true. He was in a band that started out in the late 1970s, and still plays together today. They still honor him as he was a major part of their team and wrote many popular songs that are still played today.

This beautiful soul had a very challenging life and demons that he struggled with, and those demons brought about an early death for him. When this beautiful young man passed away in 1991, it was announced on the radio, and my heart and my soul was broken. I felt the pain as he lived through his challenges, and I felt the pain when he passed. I know he is at peace now and all is forgiven.

Steve comes to me in this life and shows himself to me and gives me the look that says that he remembers our past life and the bond we had together. He knows the song that I chose in this lifetime that connects me to him. The songs he wrote and put together are ones he knows have always been hard for me to listen to, but I listen anyway.

The connection with him in this lifetime enables me to tell you what he felt like when he was living on this earth most recently. He was happy on the outside and terrified and lost and in a lot of pain on the inside. His dad was not much help. They bumped heads. Nothing he did was ever good enough for his father to be proud of him. He was a beautiful, sweet soul with a big heart, and was extremely shy. He went after his dreams, and they came true even for a short time.

As I was growing up in this life, people would ask if I was Irish/Gaelic or British, as I would speak with a slight accent that would find its way out at times. I would say no, I am not. So, my past life came with me into this life, which I find very cool. I took an ancestry DNA test in 2020 and found that I am 3% Irish, and I am English as well. How funny is that?

I love it when Steve comes to me and visits. I can see him walking around with that beautiful smile and long blond hair. It's really cool when he comes, literally through my body, like an ocean wave – just amazing.

He would love for me to get a message to his bandmates, but I highly doubt I could get that close to them. But if I ever get the chance, I will relay the messages he has for them, especially Phil, because my friend gets extremely concerned about him and the thoughts he has in his head about Steve.

Steve will always be sorry for leaving Phil the way he did and making him second-guess his own mentality at times. He has shown me a special place he and Phil loved when they first started out and played locally. They both have grand memories of that place.

People never really leave us when they die. They are always there, and that again is teamwork. That's the only way to work in the world. It's like making a cake. You have several ingredients, and if you leave a few out, the recipe doesn't work. Likewise, we must work together and accomplish what we are here to do.

Steve, it's a pleasure to have known you and work with you, my buddy, and to still be able to connect with you. R.I.P., STEVE – THE RIFFMASTER!

The Confederate Soldier

The next past life I remember was when I was a Confederate soldier in the Civil War. I was a young man from the Deep South with dark, dark hair, a light-to-medium skin tone, and dark eyes.

I could be a rebel, and extremely stubborn, to the point where it would backfire on me most of the time. The Irish must have traveled with me to the Civil War times.

In the two past lives above, the pattern was about teamwork, but in this one there was a slight change. As my stubborn behavior took over, I found myself separated from my troop. As I traveled alone in a wooded area it started to rain, sleet, and snow just enough to make it slippery.

I continued to travel onwards, deeper into the wooded area. I came to a hill, stopped, and assessed the area by listening, looking, and using my gut instincts. I knew I had traveled a bit too far, but still, I didn't stop. I was in full uniform, with a hat, canteen, rifle, and bedroll.

I ended up slipping down the hill and puncturing my right leg and knee area and breaking my left arm. I saw the damage and I knew this wasn't going to end well, that no one would find me, as my troop had gone in the opposite direction. If I had listened to what I was told to do, I would have been with my troop, my team, working together, but with my bad behavior I somehow went solo for a bit to cool off and ended up dying on a hill.

In this life now, my right knee has occasional odd pains and I have obviously brought this injury from that past life to this life now. I feel this is a reminder that stubbornness is never the way to go. No one is above the other. Working as a team gets you to the water you need to drink.

In this life now, I have always been drawn to the Deep South. When I was working at my first job, I remember customers asking me where in the South I was from and saying how they loved my Southern accent. I was like, "I was born here in Connecticut with a New England accent," and they wouldn't believe me. It's obvious to me that I brought my Southern accent and injury with me to this life.

For many years, I have been wanting to go back to the Deep South. I don't mean Florida, though. I don't consider Florida as part of the Deep South. More likely I was from the Georgia or Louisiana area. Growing up, I would get very depressed over a place I had never been to and didn't know much about other than what I had read or heard. Having been a Confederate soldier from the South would explain why I felt this way.

Past Life with My Spirit Guide, Steve

My next past life is very, very interesting and totally amazing as it is with one of my spirit guides, Steve.

I will reveal how I met two beautiful, loving, sweet, hilarious, *LOUD* but gentle and very protective of me souls, Steve and Jim, later. I have had many past lives with these boys. I call them MY BOYS because that is exactly who they are, and they love that I address them in that way. It makes them feel very loved and that someone is listening and hearing them unlike when they were on this earth. Trust is EVERYTHING to them.

Jim and Steve have had many past lives together. They were brothers in many of them, as they were in their most recent life, and just as close then as they were in this lifetime. In their previous lives, they spent all their time together, just like they did in this life. They will ALWAYS connect with each other. In fact, Jim is already making plans to come back to live on this earth with Steve and me again after I pass from this life.

Steve has shown me a life we had together back in the late 1800s. We were a young couple blessed with a sweet baby daughter. We resided in France. He showed me a river on the west side of France. It was beautiful and peaceful. We sat together as a couple on the banks along the river a lot of the time. He loved to read and was very knowledgeable about many things.

We didn't live too far from there. We would walk together to and from our home that he built for us. It was tiny and cozy, and it was all we needed to be happy. We were simple folks and very proud of what we had together.

The town was small as well. We all worked to keep the town up and running. I was known for working and helping others by using herbs and potions to help heal pain and sickness. Steve worked with his hands and mind as a wheelwright/blacksmith. He loved horses, and they loved him. They seemed to have calmed each other when in need. Working as a team was the only way to go, as those times were hard and trying.

The Family Connection

I have done many past life readings for others as far back to the times of the Crusades, which is totally amazing to me. As I see the horses, castles, dinnerware, clothing, and jewelry, I can feel the vibe of it all. The not-so-nice part of going that far back is the battles and bloodshed and death that I see. It's the same with everything there, the good and the bad that we all must endure at some point.

Having said this brings me to one of my favorite past lives, which I realized was in the late 1700s, because I saw that George Washington was the president at that time. I was a very small child, a little boy of three years old, and I was sitting with my mother as she read to me in front of the fireplace. It was cold, windy, and damp that night and very dark out, as it was raining. I could hear the horses whinnying and being somewhat restless due to the weather. She continued to read to me to calm me, as she always did. The time I spent with my mother in that past life was my favorite. We had a special bond.

That mother was also my grandmother (on my mom's side) from my own lifetime. This is complicated to explain, but here is the connection: my grandmother also had a past life – as the mother of the boy whose past life I experienced. I only wish I had met her in this life, but my grandmother died long before I was born. Those memories of my grandmother that I felt, I cherished for the rest of my life. Our home was warm and loving, and we helped whenever someone needed it.

These are just a few past lives that have stuck out to me to use in this book. There are many more, but I won't bore you too much with them. As you will see, there is a pattern which explains why my boys and I choose to use these stories, one that will help show what needs to be heard throughout our stories.

CHAPTER 4

PUTTING MY ABILITIES TO WORK

As I sit here thinking about how to lay out this chapter, I am seeing the ideas pour in, and they are coming in fast. I thank my boys Jim and Steve for that, as they are *always* on top of things. I have realized, as I look back at the pattern of things in my life and what I have experienced, I have really grown and learned a lot of life's lessons. They weren't always pleasant and happy ones but that is how life operates. You must take the good with the bad as it balances everything out. I see the full path and the connection of each piece of my life's puzzle of my personal journey from the beginning.

From being a very shy child to an adult, my gifts brought me out of my comfort zone at full speed, with many emotions all rolled into one mind, body, and soul. In this lifetime, I have had a wonderful life with such loving, caring, hard working parents, husband, and children. They have always had my back and been extremely supportive of me. They didn't always have the answers, but who does, really? Looking back, I am glad they didn't have all the answers. This way I got to wander and explore on my own what I needed to bring me to the person I am today.

In this chapter, I will share with you some of my personal experiences I have had on this amazing, wild, and crazy ride as I learned and accepted my abilities as a psychic, a medium, and a remote healer in order to help others achieve what they need to through online chat readings, as well as helping other psychics mediums in the beginning stages of understanding their intuition and coming to feel comfortable in their own minds, bodies, and souls.

In this chapter, I will share with you how my abilities came about and how I put together a self-portrait of my spiritual side along with my everyday life as a stay-at-home mom. I will share the emotions, thoughts, fears, and worries I had.

Would they think I was crazy or weird? Would they be standoffish? Would they be judgmental?

Would they be afraid of me? Would I lose friends? family? Would I make New friends? Would they accept my new ideas? Would there be jealousy?

Will I have a whole new life with what I know I can do and have done and will continue to do for the rest of my life? I have no control, really, as I was given these gifts for many reasons.

Many things went through my mind as I started to develop and apply my gifts in order to achieve the purpose for why I am here – which is to help Jim, Steve, and Sweetpea, *as they chose me to be their anchor and voice to this earthly realm, to help them get their story out and to be heard, because they need peace as well, along with many other innocent people.*

As I mentioned earlier, I had a great childhood and young adulthood. Then I met and married the man of my dreams. We decided to start a family and I became a stay-at-home mom with two children. I was blessed by being able to stay at home. It was not easy to do it, but I am very grateful I did. For us, it was a little easier, as we are frugal people.

Expensive materialistic things never mattered to us. What was important was that our children had their parents at home with them, and that mattered more to us than money. I loved staying home with the children. We raised our family in a small country town in Ellington, Connecticut, located in Tolland County. We had our good times and hard times, as everyone does, and we got through them all as a family. Remember, teamwork is the key, as we all must do our part in every situation in life to make this world go around.

I also got to spend a lot of time with my parents. They really enjoyed our kids, as they did with all their grandchildren. The part I really, really did not enjoy was when Dad got sick and passed away in March 2015. This broke my heart. It has been eight years, and it still feels raw. He was my rock. If anyone understood me it was him, and if he didn't have the answers somehow the connection between us did. He helped me when he was living and continues to assist me as a soul in heaven. *This bond will not and cannot be broken.* I will always be grateful for my dad.

My mom also passed away, in February 2020. This was devastating to me as well, and it too still feels raw today. Mom was always there for me, just as Dad was. She wasn't just my mom. She was my friend. We had so many fun times together. She also got me through a lot of difficult times like a true mom would do for her child. I am so grateful for having had the most amazing parents anyone could have.

When my children were little, I was always busy tending to them and their needs, as any mother would. I didn't notice much of my abilities at all during that time, as they were in a dormant stage, if you will, although I never forgot about them. I was still very interested in learning about them and myself and what my purpose was here on this earth.

I was always intrigued by the past, and the future. I was not so interested in the present, however, as I found it was and still is hard for me to focus on the present, as my mind is always going backwards or forwards.

I have always been fascinated with how things were in the past. It felt like I should have been there as I missed a place I have never been to. The sadness was always intense for me.

The future is the same. Again, I have never been there – *yet* – but I often felt I had to rush to get somewhere I never knew or had been to, because I missed it greatly.

There was never any middle ground or gray area, just a black or white, all-or-nothing type of living, as I like to call it.

As my children grew a little older and were in school full time, I had some more of the pieces I needed to put more of the puzzle together. I just didn't know how to go about it or what order they needed to be placed in. I realized that the pieces I did have were the outside pieces, the border of my puzzle, so I put them together to form, little by little, the information I needed to make the connection to learn about myself and how I would factor all of this into my everyday life.

As I pieced the border together, I noticed that my puzzle had a lot of darkness and a lot of rainbow colors, like the at-first confusing middle pieces of a jigsaw puzzle – pieces that meant I would have to question all of this as I went along putting this puzzle together. I knew I had to find more pieces, and understand the pieces, and accept how they were to fit together to make my understanding complete.

While the children were attending school full time, my gifts started to reopen and expand and would occur in a more consistent manner. I would notice this more because it was quieter around me, so I was able to see and hear what was going on. Things started to happen in a different way or maybe in an additional way.

I would drive to places to do my errands and go about my days, then, suddenly, I saw the same place where I was but in another time. It was my hometown in Ellington, Connecticut, but in the 1800s. I could see the people that were walking around and riding in their buggies, I could hear the clickety-clack and smell the horses and feel the wind from that time. People were having conversations and going about their business. I could see and hear them, but they couldn't see or hear me. I would see the actual locals that lived here then. I thought, *Oh my god! What literally just happened and how did this happen?*

I knew that if I told anyone, they would think I was going insane. That's what frightened me the most. In this lifetime, my family loved to go to the town green for many different reasons, such as prom night, holiday events, and other community gatherings.

One Memorial Day, we went to the service that was being held at the high school, and they had a list of the deceased soldiers from our town and said a few words about each of them. As I was sitting there, I felt my head forced to look to the left, and I saw this person who had a loved one in town die in one of the wars. As I sat there and listened, I started to see and hear visions of the bombs, the planes, and tents. These soldiers were attacked in their tent and killed, and this spirit was telling me his story. I could taste the dirt, smell the burning, and see the bombs hit these young men.

This spirit then turned my head to a person on the other side of the room to let me know that she was his sister and he wanted to get a message to her. I started to write down on the pamphlet the information he was giving me such as the year and place. There was a list of the local soldiers that had been killed, and he took the pen and circled his name for me.

When I got home, I Googled all the information he had given me and found what he had told me. I also found out that his sister lived four houses away from me. How crazy is that! I did make a few attempts to contact her, but I didn't know how she would feel about this, as you never know where people are in the healing process.

After the service, we went outside and found a spot to stand for the parade that was about to begin. There are many historical homes here in this area, and as I was looking around, waiting for the parade to start, I saw a cowboy from the 1800s. He was tall and thin, almost frail-like, wearing a hat, and wiping his boots off outside his doorstep before he entered his home through the side door. I was amazed. Now, as I drive through town and pass this house, I often see this man standing outside his home, smoking and waiting for someone to arrive.

Another interesting vision I have received many times is a short old man in overalls, with gray/white stringy hair, carrying large stones from one side of the yard to his front yard where his house stood on the main road. He was building a wall and steps in front of his home. He looked like he was crotchety, lonely, and set in his ways. His energy felt sad. The house is now gone as of a few years back, but the wall and stairs remain, and I still see him shuffling along, carrying the large stones as I sit at the light at the intersection where his home once stood.

I have also been in contact with the local dentist/doctor from that time at his home with his family. I see this quite often. It wasn't only in Ellington I would see the past, but the surrounding towns as well. The next town over, Vernon, has a very dark and heavy vibe to it. For me, it's very hard to go through that town because I get many visions of not-so-nice things. I always see a young blond girl being kidnapped by two men. She was drugged and driven to another location. This is very hard to watch, and I have had this vision over and over many times. This young female soul had me pull over so she could tell me what happened to her. The information that she gave me was very disturbing.

At this time in my life, visions were coming at me at a rapid pace. I was trying to take them all in and figure out what I was seeing, why I was seeing them, and who they were. It scared me at first as I didn't know much about visions. I felt the need to start taking pictures, and I felt the need to look closely at these pictures after I took them. What I would find were orbs and faces. Even when I took pictures of homes, I could see the people I saw in front of me in the town from the 1800s.

I took my pictures to the Nellie McKnight House/ Ellington Historical Society, and two of the ladies were very intrigued at what I showed them, as they knew who those faces were in my pictures. That's how clear the faces were that I captured. I was nudged to continue to take pictures and videos, and I would capture the most amazing things and people, but also not-so-nice things. Like I said above, you must take the good with the bad, and I have had my share of the bad. As I continued to take these pictures and videos, I found so much in them. It was a relief that others saw what I saw, and even better when they knew who the people were. That was super cool! I did this for a long time, and still do this today, as I know now it is a part of who I am and what I am here to do.

Another example I would like to share is when I was driving past Crystal Lake/Sandy Beach in Ellington. Suddenly, a young girl with messy, bloody hair walked in front of my car and crossed the road. She looked at me and said, *"Help me!"* and vanished. I thought, *OMG! What is going on?!* At Crystal Lake/ Sandy Beach, I saw many young girls with wet bloody and messy hair, wearing torn clothes as the kids and I spent many summers there.

These incidents happened all the time. At first, I was afraid to tell anyone because I didn't know how they would react, especially my family and extended family. What would they think of me? So many things entered my mind. I kept a lot of this to myself for a very long time.

I started to investigate why all this was happening in my life. It had happened to me as far back as age five. I remember things I saw and still see, things that no one else was seeing or hearing. I always had to know everything, why, when, and how things were going to happen. I love surprises, but I also love to know when and how things will be laid out and come to fruition. I used to call it being nosy, but with the intense feelings I had, I knew it was more than that.

There was a reason for all this and why it was happening to me. I had to find out who I was, as I have always felt lost and invisible, and having been shy didn't help. I had to find out, not for the sister in me, the aunt, the mother, or the wife, but for *me* as an individual human being.

At this time, the experiences were still coming at full speed. As I mentioned prior to this chapter, I was always fascinated with psychics and mediums, and with death. I find it very cool to communicate with the other side, to get messages, to find out about the future, and to receive answers to unanswered questions and thoughts, as well as guidance and direction.

I started to go to different psychics around me, as I had to understand what was coming up. I didn't know how they got their information, but they knew what was going on with me without me saying a word. I also noticed that each one I went to did things differently, and I thought, *Hmm... how can that be?* I would put all the information I received in the back of my mind to pull out later, to consider where things would fit in with that puzzle I was solving, and if they were really going to unfold in the way that these people said things would. I wondered, *how do you do that - how do you know such things?* I knew it was really happening because some of them have brought messages for me from my dead loved ones, and they were spot-on.

I was very impressed, except with one local psychic medium. I saw her as being rude to spirits, loud, overpowering, obnoxious, and full of herself - not to mention very unorganized. Her ego was and is too large for herself, and her readings were *never* spot-on or even close. She never cleanses after readings, which leaves all the debris of the previous readings' remains on her and transfers them to the next client. She does this for a living and to gain attention and money. Her heart is not in it for the right reasons, as she abuses her gifts for all the wrong reasons and manipulates others to get them to her side and to believe and support her. I never went back to her and never will.

As I spoke to all the other psychic mediums, they all confirmed that I was indeed a psychic and a medium, and that I should investigate it and putting myself and my abilities to work. So, I did.

I started to read a lot on my own to try to understand what gifts I have and to try to make sense of things. I bought many books, and they seemed to help me maneuver in the direction I needed to go. I knew my life was about to change. I just didn't know how much at that time, as I wasn't prepared for what I was about to go through on this wild and crazy, amazing ride my intuition was about to bring me on. What I was about to learn and experience was not in any books *until this one.*

As I continued to focus on raising our children and learning about my abilities, I was finding some great information as I read the descriptions of all the types of abilities and how they matched me to a T. I was very excited yet overwhelmed, as I still had to figure out how to put all this together to make things work.

In March of 2015 I had to say goodbye to my dad, my rock, the one that understood me the most, when he passed away. This was a very, very hard time for me. The pain was massive and surreal. The last time I saw him say goodbye on this earth, he just didn't look like himself, but I can understand that. I touched his hands, and he moved his hands to touch mine back as a sign that he will always be with me. I stepped back wondering, *Did this just really happen?* I thought I would never see my dad again, but never say never, as all things are possible.

I went to a psychic medium hoping to connect with my dad after he passed, and he came through right away. I could not believe what I was seeing, hearing, and feeling. I saw him in full figure for about eight seconds. It takes a massive amount of energy for spirits to do this. I was amazed. The first two things he said was that "I did everything right for him" and

"There is a God, he is real." He walked over to me and gave me a hug from the back (I was sitting at a table). For the rest of the reading, my left thumb was moving wildly. I had no control over it. This was dad moving my thumb, letting me know he was still there. This is his way to communicate with me. It's our connection from heaven to earth.

I found that once my dad had passed away, the sensations and happenings I had been feeling increased even more. I couldn't understand why until I learned that once a loved one passes on, they will help you from the other side and help open your intuition. I felt my dad around all the time, and I would smell the soap and Chapstick he used.

One day, I went out with the kids to put them on the bus, and when I came back to the door there was a long line of pennies from the bottom of the stairs to the top. I knew Dad had made a visit. I thought this was crazy, yet amazing. I continue to receive signs from Dad and I love every one of them. When he leaves dimes and pennies, they have the date of 2015 on them, the year he passed.

That was when I started to take more pictures and videos as I was drawn and nudged to do it. When I viewed them, I found many times that my dad's face was in the orbs or just in the picture itself. I was prodded to take a selfie, and when I looked at it, my dad was in the picture too.

I have also seen other family members, such as my husband's father and grandmother. His grandmother comes as a red cardinal when she visits, and when I take a picture of the cardinal, her face is there, always next to the cardinal.

Another incident of this was when we were visiting a friend, my husband's uncle was sick and ready to pass at any time. I was sitting on the couch and having a conversation then, suddenly, I saw a male spirit standing across the room. I saw the word UNCLE pass my eyes repeatedly like a lit, neon sign in a restaurant or bar just flashing and scrolling. I leaned over to him and said, "Your uncle passed, and he is here to say goodbye." My husband wasn't sure what to think. When we got back to the car, there was a message on his phone, that he had left in the car, telling us that his uncle had indeed passed away. The other crazy thing was that when we saw the memorial card, I realized that his uncle was wearing the same outfit as when he appeared to me to relay his message.

This was a time that overwhelmed me a lot, as things continued to escalate at a rapid pace. I feared what my husband thought, as most people are not open to the spiritual side of things. Many people react doubtfully or badly, as they are scared to know about connecting to heaven, and how it's done and what happens. It's the fear in people and ignorance that stop them from knowing, which I can totally understand, but you can't let fear and worry control you. You need to make it work for you, like anxiety, and use it as motivation.

Use fear to run or use fear to rise. I choose to rise.

As I learned more about the spirit world and how to channel with the other side, I found that there is more than one way to do this. I wasn't out of my comfort zone yet at this time, but I knew I had to keep moving forward and learn and experience more as it came to me. It became very overwhelming.

I tried to share this with others, and they were not receptive at all. I felt I could trust these people, but found out that I really couldn't, because they just continued to belittle me and project their own feelings towards me even more. They thought I was making things up, off my rocker, losing my mind, and couldn't understand why I was pursuing this. It turned out that it was their jealousy that was causing a lot of their negative behaviors.

I let their behavior bother me for a little while, but not much longer than that, as true colors really do come out eventually. I felt many different emotions for a long time, but I knew I was right. Dealing with all that, I became sad, angry, depressed, scared, confused, negative, cranky, mean; all the things I knew I wasn't. I didn't want to feel this way anymore. I had to figure things out more and place things in order and start putting more of the pieces of the puzzle in place.

Things started to make sense to me and were spot-on. All the unanswered questions were starting to be answered. I was understanding more and getting used to the things that were happening. I thought about taking classes on how to handle and control all of this but remembered what the psychics I talked with all said, *"No, you don't need classes,"* that I was way above classes, and to just follow my intuition, so I continued to do so.

As I continued to see the towns as they used to be and hear and smell the horses and hear the people chattering and going about their business, I got to really love what I was experiencing. How often does this happen to people? Why? I always felt things happen for a reason no matter what happened and to whom. In my mind, there are no coincidences.

I started to put more pieces of the puzzle together and to get a visual glimpse of what I needed to know and where I was to go with all this. I have always been a visual person. Now I know why – it's the clairvoyant in me! As my third eye opens more and more, and it does, it shows me things in detail. The third eye is an invisible eye that is located on the forehead between the eyebrows. It provides perception beyond ordinary sight to where I can see the visions that are sent to me. I started to follow my clairvoyance first, along with claircognizance – *the ability of knowing.*

As I focused on these to start with, I practiced with my friends, and found that I was spot-on and that there would be no way of me knowing any of the information I had, as it was only their private information to know. I started to ponder how I could keep practicing this. A thought popped into my head to make a website on Facebook and start practicing readings with strangers.

This was way out of my comfort zone, as I was still on the shy side. I asked a friend what she thought of me doing this, and her response was *"Go for it! You have what it takes to be successful."* As I got to know my abilities, I became very comfortable with the experiences.

This had been going on now for a few years at this intense stage, so it was becoming second nature to me. I began seeing spirit children and young teens, males and females, and they were from different eras: the 1960s, 1970s, and 1980s through the present. I had no idea why I was seeing them all over the place other than that they were trying to get my attention because they wanted to tell their stories. It wasn't in a consistent pattern, just here and there – *for the time being.*

In 2017, I started my own business, called Hearing from Heaven – Psychic Medium Online Chat Readings, which can be found on Facebook. I made a business page for people to contact me for readings, and I would advertise as well. I was playing around with this for a while and trying different things. It was around the holidays when I started this, so I created games with which to attract clients, such as guess how many crystals or stones are in the jar for a free reading. I really enjoyed doing things like that, as it gave me a chance to practice my gifts and help others – a win-win. This brought me even further out of my comfort zone. I was offering free readings for many, many months to get used to the pattern of things and the amount of time it required. Longer readings can be exhausting, so I started small and increased my services as I went along.

I have met so many beautiful souls in all sorts of situations. One person I met was my soulmate and soul sister. I mentioned her in an earlier chapter. Her name is Stevie. She has been by my side since I started Hearing from Heaven. She has been extremely supportive, understanding, and helpful in many more ways than she knows. In return, I have helped her understand herself, as she too was starting to get a feel for her own psychic medium abilities.

She says I mentored her, but I feel we mentored each other. We both have totally different styles, which is cool, because we can combine our gifts and get to the root of the issues for a client if need be. We can even have a three-way reading chat, as we both work from home and are available to each other without judgment. We are sisters in more ways than one, and blood is not one of the ways. *I will always cherish and feel grateful and blessed for knowing Stevie.*

I have read for many, many people, both locally and internationally. I find it amazing how many depend on psychics for guidance and direction. I think it's wonderful that they treat readings like a therapy session but with much more detail.

I love chatting with my clients because I get to know them like I do a friend. We build a foundation like a friendship with trust and compassion. It feels so good on so many levels to help others through tough choices, heartbreaks, and the deaths of loved ones, to mention a few. I take my abilities very seriously and I will *never* just tell someone what they want to hear. I only tell the truth as it is given to me by the Lord, spirit, my guides, my clients' guides, our loved ones, and the universe. What I love is when, after a reading, the client leaves a review, and it both tells me and shows me that I have done my job properly.

Below, I will share some of the reviews from my clients, anonymously. They all touched my heart when I was first starting out.

Reviews I Have Received

Sue is one of the sweetest people I have ever met. I highly recommend scheduling an appointment with her. She's the best!

Sue did a fantastic and very personal spot-on reading! I got goosebumps and am very impressed with her gift. She will only get stronger as she practices. I can't wait!

Sue was phenomenal, almost eerily so, but in a good way. She is sensitive and sweet, and I feel she will go a long way. She is truly blessed with a spiritual gift. 5 stars.

Sue is absolutely amazing. I can't believe how much comfort she has brought to my life since her reading. She has provided myself and my family with many answers. She is very professional and has a sweet soul. I was so nervous, and she made me feel at ease. She is a blessing. Everything she said was correct and on-point.

Sue was spot-on with the personalities of our loved ones from heaven, and I knew she was really connected. Very impressive. 5 stars

Sue has an authentic gift; her gentle nature and open heart only add to the insights she has to offer. She provided not only clarity, but comfort as well. I'd recommend her to anyone.

Thank you, Sue!

Sue was phenomenal. She helped me realize how my husband's spirit is always with me. Her clarity on events and emotions was superb. Sue has the ability to see and read into what appears. I'm sure she'll help 1,000s of people in putting their minds at ease and assisting them in moving forward. She's been blessed with a beautiful gift!!!!!

Sue is very talented & on a great journey. May you all be blessed by her insights & gifts.

Sue, you are amazing! You were spot on with your description of a past loved one. Your abilities are a gift. Thank you for the reading and I will be watching for the future events you described. Will keep you posted. Keep spreading smiles!

Sue spent a lot of time with me. She came right out with pain in my knees, which is accurate. That I am frustrated with how much it slows me down. (This

was so true.) She was correct about loved ones on the other side, especially with visual descriptions and personalities. She delivered messages in a caring way. I like that she would work with a vague question you might have. This was a positive experience. Thanks so much Sue!

Thank you so much for spending so much time with my loved ones and me. You know how much I truly appreciate your insights. I especially needed that one connection. It has given me some clarity for closure - which I needed. Thank you.

Wonderful experience! The chat experience is unique and one I will do this again. I'm very thankful for the insight and messages Susan sent me.

Had a great experience. Was my first time. She was spot on with most of the information, some things I must investigate, but overall had a good time.

Just had a spot-on reading with Sue! I was skeptical about having an online reading, but she was very informative and had me laughing and crying with some of the messages she delivered. Awesome!!

My reading was very accurate and detailed. I enjoyed hearing messages from family and friends who have passed on. I will recommend her!

This is truly a gifted and caring person. She took a long time with me and was very accurate. My reading let me know that my loved one is with me, and I am not alone. She spent her time and didn't ask for anything in return. She is a blessing.

I am amazed! She truly was right about everything that was said. Very sweet and kind. I will get another reading done!!

I really enjoyed my reading she picked up on some things right away...she was on point with many things a very kind person and easy to talk to.!!

Had a reading with Sue, and at first, I was skeptical and thought we'll see what she has to say... we'll she couldn't have been more dead-on to everything that she said, and it provided me with comfort on some things that always bothered me. I highly recommend her if you are looking to have one done!!

I have been waiting for years to hear from my grandparents. We finally connected through Hearing from Heaven yesterday. My grandfather's song to me was even brought up. So many things were validated. I was in tears. Thank you so much for sharing your gift with me.

I had an online reading with Sue, and it was so eye opening. She reconnected me with someone who I thought had, sort of, forgotten about me long ago... not so.

She was spot-on with things I'm going through and provided helpful insight. I would LOVE to talk with her again. If you get the opportunity to... I highly recommend it!

She's unlike any other psychic you will come across, she's not only honest but very compassionate! She's compassionate with those she works with; she helps you understand and restore a sense of peace! I HIGHLY RECOMMEND HER.

I have no words. Truly gifted. Hands down, the best reading I've ever had! A gift and a blessing. THANK YOU

⭐ ⭐ ⭐ ⭐ ⭐

I feel like she's right on although it was a little scary to hear. But she's right.

She is amazing! So spot-on about everything literally. Will definitely reach out to her again!

You are the best! I appreciate you so much knowing you are here for me makes me feel so safe and calm... I'm happy I did not post this review immediately after our chat because my POI did text me next day Thanksgiving... That made me feel so calm and reassured that what you told me is unfolding even though the appearance of social media is deceiving!! Love you and can't wait to chat in a few days!!

She is absolutely amazing! The way that she delivers the truth you seek is so helpful. And she sees it all.

As I re-read my reviews and feedback, it again tells me that I am doing the right thing. When you help others in the proper way, how can anything go wrong? I was amazed at myself as I read these. I kept thinking, "How do I know all these things, how is it possible?" But I knew. This made me feel wonderful and fulfilled inside.

This made me want to continue to dig in and learn the next few abilities and get to understand them and put them to work as well. I started to advertise more on my Facebook page and by setting my business cards out in public places. I was also getting creative. This was when kindness rocks were getting popular, so I made rocks that said "Hearing from Heaven" with "Free readings if you find this rock" on the back. I placed them in various places in my surrounding towns, and they were found.

I like to keep it light and happy, but with boundaries as well, as I can get bombarded with clients and spirits wanting my attention. I had to learn how to protect myself and my surroundings. I found it is extremely important to do this.

Many things can come through a reading, wanted or unwanted, and you must be prepared for both. I have had my share of the bad, creepy stuff. I send it away when it appears. I will *NOT* look into it if someone asked if anyone put a spell on them or sent bad vibes their way. I am a very *rare* and *unique* psychic medium, and I am very sensitive, as I can pick up anything anywhere, so I don't go looking for it.

This is where the boundaries come in. I don't work with spells, rituals, devil worshiping, black magic, any other magic, or anything like that. That is *NOT* what I do or who I am. I work for the Lord with the gifts He gave me to help others find their way in life. As my business started to take off and fast, I added more services to my business page. I started to do email readings, online chat readings with different time lengths, and 2-person and 3-person combination online chat readings.

Then I got very confident and offered psychic medium parties. I did this for many months and enjoyed how I got to experiment to find my style of reading. I was nervous to practice face-to-face readings, and with parties of course you would need to do this. I learned more and accepted what I had to do, and then I tried it. I went to a home in Tolland, Connecticut and I met a very nice lady and had a small practice party. We both felt it went well.

CHAPTER 5

MEETING MY SPIRIT GUIDES, JIM AND STEVE - "MY BOYS"

In my mind, there are no coincidences in life. Everything happens for a reason, whether it's a bad experience, a good experience, an easy or a hard experience. This is what life is. This is what brings you forward and conquers obstacles. There are many things to learn. If we don't learn them, we stay idle, in a rut.

Our free will lets us do that if we choose, but why would you choose not to move forward? Is it fear? Worry? Anxiety? A lack of confidence? A lack of self-esteem? Does someone have a hold on you or control your every move and thought? Are you scared of what people will think and say? There are endless reasons why we don't or won't move forward.

The most important lesson I have learned with my life experiences and with my abilities is to be who you are. Make goals and follow your dreams. Don't just sit on the sidelines and watch life go by. Be a part of it and do your job, as you are part of a team, as teamwork is what makes this world go around.

The fear of the unknown and the ignorance that people have is what stops us in our tracks. Going out of our comfort zone is the best thing we can do for ourselves, because it will help us grow in many ways, gain knowledge, and help others to move forward as well.

In this chapter I will be introducing my spirit guides, Jim and Steve, along with a few other lessons I had to endure in my journey to get to where I am today.

I used these times as steppingstones to move along on my path. Some are larger and longer than others, but they all get you to the destination you are meant to reach. I had a few close, wonderful friends who helped me through a hard, difficult time where I had to take a few steps back to move forward.

During this time, I had to work in retail for a bit in a local CVS to get by financially while starting my business. I also sought another job with an online company in New Zealand called Lifereader.com and another with Keen.com. These are sites where psychic mediums work as advisors and offer online chat readings. I absolutely love these sites. I have had many, many clients from all over the world, which I feel is cool. I've met and formed a foundation and a relationship with many clients, and with other advisors.

Working three jobs and never having been in retail before was something I found to be an exhausting challenge, but I worked with a great group of people who helped keep me going. I feel very grateful for having had that job. I even started to read for the customers. I would see spirits enter the store with the customers and realize that they were their loved ones following them on their day-to-day routines. I felt this was pretty darn cool.

There was a photo center in CVS, and when I worked with the photos and got the orders together, I would notice orbs in them. When the customer came to pick them up, I found myself giving them messages from their loved ones. They really appreciated the messages, as they were spot-on. This made me feel good, as everyone needs to be heard, living or dead. I found myself doing this daily.

One thing that happened was extremely interesting and crazy. One day, as I was working upstairs putting products away, I felt a breeze pass me and I heard small feet running. I saw a flash of a little girl playing around and pushing the products off the shelves. It was hilarious, watching her do this, many times over, upstairs and on the floor. I would catch her kneeling, looking at the baby aisle and the toys. She also had company with her. It was her dad, a large man with heavy feet – so when he was around, you knew it. His energy was cranky, and he was set in his ways, and you knew you didn't want to mess with this man.

I started to see them on a regular basis. Once, he ran down the stairs at me, and his energy was strong and loud. I could also see him peeking through the ceiling tiles through the second floor (some were missing).

I would talk to them during my shifts. I asked why they were there, and they told me their story. They showed me that this CVS was once a gas station. I could see the old pumps with the pinkish hoses. He was dressed in a mechanic's uniform, and all dirty and greasy, as any mechanic and/or gas station owner would be. He told me that there was an explosion, and he was caught in it with his daughter, who was visiting that day. She had died first. He had felt guilt and shame ever since, and they both refused to cross over. I would see him in the parking lot as well, because he would walk the grounds that were once part of the property around his business.

They loved to wreak havoc, and I thought it was hilarious. When the summer products were out, there would be balls in the aisles, the register drawers would open, the front doors would go wild, and our drinks would dump over. My coworkers would experience some of these things, but they said it increased when I started working there. *Imagine that!!!* I told them the story and they understood (well, most of them), but some would never go back upstairs – LOL!

I really enjoyed working there, as it taught me a lot, and gave me strength and more self-confidence and self-esteem. I continued to work at CVS with the goal of doing my readings full time. Staying at CVS was really hard, as the hours were different each week and some were overnights and weekends. It started to wear on me, exhausting me to the bone, as I also had my Lifereader.com and Keen.com jobs. I did prove to myself that I could handle anything that is thrown at me, and that even if I fall, I will always get up and move forward on my path.

One night, I was lying in bed asleep when I was woken up by someone floating above me. I could not believe who I was seeing. It was the *Lord Jesus Christ* himself. I thought, *WOW, am I really seeing him?* The comfort he brought me was out of this world. He reached down to me, touched my face, smiled, and said *"My daughter, you will work for me now,"* I just couldn't believe this. I thought, *Should I tell anyone, or not?* I kept it to myself for a while. But I did share it later. I also saw *Mary, the mother of Jesus,* while working on Lifereader.com – I glanced over to my right, and I saw her standing there briefly. She smiled, nodded, and faded away. Again, I questioned, *Did I just see her too?*

This was amazing, I couldn't find the words for what I was experiencing. There are none! I was thinking, *Okay, now I've seen both back-to-back within a few weeks apart, so there must be a reason. What was it? Why me? Is it because the Lord gave me my gifts and he was checking on me? Was Mary there to offer motherly support?* For the next few weeks, I listened to my intuition much more closely than I had in the past since the Lord himself said I would work for him now, and waited to see if I would get any signs or dreams of any kind that would give me clues as to what was happening.

When they came to visit me, it was the calmest, most relaxed feeling I have ever had. It felt warm and loving beyond belief. I wish it had lasted longer. Maybe someday they will come back. Little did I know that this was part of the wild and crazy ride that my intuition was taking me on. What came next was even more unbelievable.

At this time, I was still learning everything I needed to know. I didn't have all the answers, but I went with my intuition on everything. As I mentioned earlier, every psychic medium has their own style of doing things. Some use tarot cards or oracle cards; some use playing cards, stones, or pendulums; others only read into certain areas. We follow our instincts and go from there.

It's the same with doctors. Would you go to an ENT for foot issues? No! You would need to seek a podiatrist, so you would choose from that specialty, establish a relationship, look for a great bedside manner, and make sure that they listen well and really care about patients ahead of their profits.

It's the same thing with choosing a psychic medium. When clients choose a psychic, we must lay the foundation and inspire trust that all readings are confidential.

What I also found out is that it's the same for spirits when they choose a psychic medium to help them. They look for a personal quality, compassion, and loving manner in a psychic medium, and for the dedication they will need them to have to get the job done. They look at how we present information and messages to a person or loved one. No one wants to have a bad experience with any doctor or with any psychic medium, or with anyone for that matter, but it does happen. It's about treating people right and with respect and respecting their boundaries.

I see and feel that *most* psychic mediums work as a team. We each have a different style, and it's what makes each of us unique. Teamwork, again, is very important in life, as it is what makes the world go around. If we all just worked together, the world would be a better place. *Are you starting to see a pattern here with teamwork?*

As spirits choose their psychic medium, they are very careful as to who they choose. There are some unethical ones out there, and fake ones, as with anything else. There are many spirits that share some visions, small bits of information with a psychic, but it's only general information until they find the right fit. If they are not comfortable or feel leery of that psychic medium's actions, they will stay clear.

Spirits will make sure they have the right person to do what they need done. I bring this up now because I feel it is extremely important to have the right people for the right jobs. Not everyone is right for every job. You must have the right background and mindset, and the motivation to follow through.

With me, I find myself working on something until it is complete. I don't leave things unfinished. That is *not* how I do things. I follow through and stay on top of the issue, just as I have with learning and controlling my intuition. Follow through, and you will get to the destination you are aiming for.

It's not always in the time frame we want, but it's in the time frame the universe wants. Hence, the sayings: *"Timing is everything"* and *"All in due time."* Patience goes together with this, like anxiety and depression, fear and worry/guilt, love and war, good and bad, heaven and hell. This is teamwork as well, just in different forms.

November 11, 2019, is a date that I will *never, ever* forget. I was home just after I had finished a shift at CVS, and I was doing a few hours of readings on Lifereader.com. I started to hear loud banging noises on the walls and floor. It sounded like boxes being dragged across a wooden floor. After I finished up with my readings, I was trying to relax after a long day of work. As I continued to hear those loud knocking noises, I was like, "What the heck? I just want to relax."

As these noises continued for days, I thought, "Okay, someone really wants my attention." I listened to these noises and the bangs of boxes dragging for days. One night, I sat quietly and listened as I heard the noises again. I heard the words *"watch, look"* over and over. So, I quietly waited and looked around and listened.

Then my hands started to move on their own. They were very fidgety and restless. I had no control of them. They started to make letters and symbols. My right hand was working alone, but it also felt like my left hand was standing by, waiting for its turn. My right hand kept making a gun with my thumb and index finger and putting it to my head. I wasn't expecting that, but it really caught my attention.

This spirit did it a few times. I asked, "Did you die by suicide?" and my left hand gave a thumbs up *as if* to confirm that this spirit did die by suicide, from a gunshot wound to his head.

Suddenly both my hands started to make the middle finger sign. Now, this got me laughing. At this point, I had no clue where this was going. Then I saw my dad appear, and he nodded his head as confirmation that it was okay to trust these two spirits, because they had some information to share with me. Once I saw my dad, I knew it would be okay for me to proceed.

I started to hear the words *"write with me"* over and over. I was like, *"Okay????"* So, I grabbed a pen and a notebook, sat on the bed, and laid the notebook in front of me with the pen next to it. I waited and waited. My hands started to get restless and fidgety, and I had no control again. Finally, my right hand grabbed the pen and started writing. The two words this spirit wrote were, *"Jim here."* I was flabbergasted. I couldn't believe what I had witnessed. Then he wrote more, and it said *"with my brother, Steve."*

I instantly felt the warmth and calm and overwhelming love that flowed from them both. It felt like I had known them forever; the overwhelming connection was electrifying. I have never felt like this before with any spirit. It was very different from any other spirit I have met. I just can't explain it in words, as there are none for this.

The whole night, I was flabbergasted. I couldn't sleep, as my mind was racing with many thoughts. I wanted to know who these brothers were and why they were coming to me. They were not showing me visions or telling me anything yet. It felt different than when the soldier came to me on Memorial Day and showed me and told me his story. Steve and Jim's energy was different, more loving, caring, and protective and familiar.

I left the notebook and pen out on my bed, and this is when the psychic writing started for me. The brothers would wake me up and want to write, and boy did they write. They were writing things and drawing pictures of things that made no sense to me at the time. The writing was happening daily, day and night. I got to know the signs when they wanted to write with me.

The boys would wake me up and I could feel them put my glasses on my face and put the pen in my hand. They can move energy well. I knew as we continued to write – and I mean write a lot – that they trusted me with the information they were about to give to me and show me. The visions were coming in slowly but started to be consistent. A story was beginning to peel away from the heavy layers it was held together with.

I felt such a great, rare connection to them both. I felt their intense pain and grief, their losses, sadness, anger, the agitation they had, the guilt, the fear, the embarrassment, and the disappointments that they had here on this earth. I knew I had to find out who these boys were and why they came to me for help. As I continued to write with them, my parents and Godmother also would write private messages to me, which I thought was more than amazing. At this point, I was learning more every day about being a psychic and a medium.

I would find that these two boys were with me everywhere I went. They would come to work with me at CVS, and they loved riding in the car with me and listening to the radio. They would send messages and signs to me with music.

These boys love communicating with me through music. I love riding around in the car just so that they can listen to the music they love. I have noticed a pattern of songs and bands, and I will share them as I go.

There was one song I noticed that would come on the car radio a lot. When I lived briefly in Tolland, Connecticut, I noticed this song would come on a lot, called *"The Boys Are Back in Town,"* a 1976 song by Thin Lizzy. I knew this was a massive clue, as it became a pattern. They then shared with me that they had lived in Tolland, CT. I got to know what music they liked and let them listen to it even if I didn't care for it. I started to take notes about all the information I received.

One thing that I found hysterically funny was how they acted like brothers. They would beat each other up and mess around like brothers do, and one time when they did this, they made such a ruckus that I thought my front door was going to break and the doorbell would never shut off. At that time, they were outside, and I was sitting at the kitchen table, and they wanted to get my attention.

Another time they really had me cracking up was at CVS. I would walk around the floor in the aisles doing my work. If they thought a customer was rude or obnoxious, they would let me know by making middle-finger gestures with my hands. I had to hide my hands quite often. I couldn't believe it. If I didn't see and feel it myself, I would say, *"No way!"*

By this time, I knew the boys were here with me to stay. They have become a part of me and my life in many, many ways. One night, we were writing, and they started to give information about a local woman who went missing from The Olive Garden next to CVS. What they wrote matched the information I heard in the store afterward.

After my shift on the Saturday night before Thanksgiving in November 2019, I stopped by the police department with the information I had received.

I started to explain to the officer the visions I was seeing and what was written in my books.

I ended up being with the police for about two hours sharing what I saw in my visions. I got the police officers to join me as I started to run through the woods along the river, like it was daytime in an empty field. The boys were showing me the way. It was getting dark and cold and there was a massive snowstorm coming the next day.

The police officers wanted to turn back, but I said, *"No! We are close to her. We just need to go about another mile, and you will see where she is."* The police *refused* to listen and brought everyone back inside.

I explained, *"If you don't go another mile, she will be carried by the current of the river and will be moved further south."* This made no difference. They wanted to stop. The next day I spoke with the detective in charge, and I explained to him again that they would have found her that night if they had listened. They went back to where we were before the storm started and found nothing. That's because they *refused* to go past where I said. They didn't see the need to go beyond a certain area.

I gave them all the information that I had been given in detail down to her fingernails and license plate and make and model of the car of the people that took her. I also explained what had happened to her physically, because she had been tortured beyond belief. They did nothing to follow up with this.

This woman was not found until a few months later, exactly where I said she would end up if they didn't find her that night. This sweet woman came to me as a spirit right after they found her body and wrote in my book: *"Thank you for your efforts."*

This again is about teamwork. If the police had listened to the things I said, things would have been different. I find that the police feel threatened by psychic mediums. They shouldn't be, as we all need to work together as a team to get the same result whether it's good or bad.

What was weird about this was that my mom passed away in February 2020, so she and this woman were in the same funeral home next to each other and had back-to-back services.

I continued to work at CVS, exhausting as it was. I enjoyed working there because it taught me independence and courage, which gave me strength to stand up for myself and set boundaries. I found so much more about myself, and again worked with many good people. These people believed in me and supported me when others did not. There are lessons in everything we do in life, and once you learn and accept them, things run much smoother.

At this time, I was also getting to know the boys more – who they were, where they were from, why they came to me. These boys are truly amazing souls. One night I was sitting quietly, listening and connecting with them. They love to write and use sign language, which

I know nothing about other than the middle finger, thumbs up, the peace sign, and the gun. It dawned on me that they were showing me the way in my journey and teaching me how to be a psychic and a medium and how to grow with my intuition, control it, and live with it in my own mind, body, and soul. They are my mentors.

As I got to know them better, my heart just started to break over and over as I learned their stories and how their lives were disrupted here on earth. It angers and pains me that people have to go through such things. It shouldn't be this way. No one should be treated the way they were treated.

These two precious souls became *my life*. I have seen both in full figure now. They are truly amazing with how they both move energy, and each one moves it so differently. They are truly unique. I see them every day, I hear them every day, they help me on many levels every day. They keep me balanced and grounded, and when I slip, they surely will remind me and put me back in place. I am extremely blessed and grateful to have them in my life. I am proud to call these two beautiful souls *"my spirit guides, my boys!"* as they chose me to be their voice on this earth to tell their story.

CHAPTER 6

GETTING TO KNOW "MY BOYS"

Getting to know "my boys" has been an exciting adventure for me and a confusing and sad one as well. But again, you need that balance of things to keep moving. I have been taking a lot of notes on what I have been seeing, hearing, and feeling from my boys.

I found that I had two puzzles to complete – not only the one for my journey, but for Jim and Steve's as well. I'm still very unsure at this time as to where they are leading me, but I do know we will figure it out together as a team and I trust them with my life. Remember, teamwork is the key.

As I sit and connect with Jim and Steve, whether it's through writing, visions, video, or audio, I truly value the time I spend with them. I talk with them all day long, and I know I can drive them nuts at times with my human actions, but they are so very patient and understanding with me as I learn from them.

They truly are very interesting souls with many hidden truths, including pain and suffering as well as happiness in their lifetime. They have shared with me some of their favorite memories and adventures that they hold close to their hearts, as much as they can.

This chapter will be about how my boys are boys and brothers and how they enjoy all that goes with it. The love they had and have for each other can *never* be broken. They had hard times, good times, sad times, scary times, and many traumas. They leaned on each other to get through anything and everything they both have endured on this earth. They have asked me to share a few memories here.

These are three of their favorite memories that were dear to them when they were really young and happy and carefree. When they showed me these sweet memories I was like, "OMG, how freaking precious is this?!" I am proud to share this for them. I would do *anything* for them, as they keep me sane on this earth on many levels with their love and protection, support, strength, laughs, and sometimes sternness. I could not endure the experiences that I have had without them, and we sure have been through some stuff, some good and some bad, dark, and creepy. There was a time they were just as scared as I was, but we made it through – *together*. No matter what it is, they are there.

The Visions

The first vision was before they moved here to Tolland, Connecticut from Torrance, California.

They were in a large field with an unpaved, dirt road on a very sunny day with a dark blue sky and only a few white puffy clouds. The breeze was warm yet refreshing. Jim had on a yellow-gold, short-sleeved shirt, which I had to giggle at because he *never* wears a shirt now. He was running like a young boy does, so carefree and happy, with no worries in the world, while his older brother Steve was running after him to tackle him. As they are showing me this vision, I can hear them laughing and giggling and yelling at each other, having fun and getting dirty and sweaty as young boys should be doing. After the tackle, they both got up and started to walk down the unpaved road, pushing each other and messing around and making fun of each other. They value the time they had back then, as they showed it to me in a very vivid and colorful scene. It's just an amazing and very sweet vision to see.

The second vision they shared with me was when they were a bit older and they were in Rhode Island, where they spent a lot of time with family and friends. I see they are getting excited as I write this – *I love it!* I get so excited to see them happy because they went through so much. They loved messing around with the neighborhood kids and cousins. They showed me a lot of people just hanging out, eating, swimming, and enjoying their time there.

The third vision they shared with me was more of a relaxing one. They were sitting on a big rock fishing and wading in the water. They looked and felt so relaxed, and I could see that they had caught some fish too. They looked so proud of themselves. I could feel the serenity in this vision, the calm and peace in their hearts as well as the love they have for each other, and I know they will always have each other's back, for eternity.

Unfortunately, my boys had a tough life. My heart hurts for them. I feel their pain, shame, guilt, sadness, anger, but also their happiness – when there was some happiness. There is no limit to what I will do for these two lovely souls.

As I sat with Jim one-on-one, I felt that he is an old, old soul. He is so passionate and patient and so loving beyond words. I never knew him in the physical sense, as he passed away at a young age, but he touched a lot of hearts when he was here on earth. He has shared with me the love he has for poetry, music, and playing the drums. I would start to see him hanging around my daughter and jamming to the tunes and playing air guitar and air drums as she played her instruments, mostly the drums too.

Jim shared that he had a band, and tried to get it moving along, but due to unforeseen circumstances, sadly, that was not brought to fruition for him. His drum set was quaint, and per Jim I had to use that word. He cherished them. It was his safe place, and it brought the real Jim out.

He really, really loves The Doors. He showed me he had a past life with Jim Morrison, and that they had similar looks – *Hot!* Their hair and mannerisms were similar, as were their thought patterns, which I found astonishing. He also loved the bands Rush and Thin Lizzy. That is probably why he always wanted to hear the song "The Boys Are Back in Town" when I would go to Tolland.

When he shows me himself, he *never* has a shirt on. He will never put a shirt on. *I love it.* He definitely has that 1970s look, jeans, long hair, and bandana. He tries to smile as much as he can for what he had to endure when he was growing up in Tolland. He also shared that he had a passion for nature and being outside, and for maple trees. They were his favorite.

Jim loved the girls, too – that is for sure. There is one he mentions all the time and how much she meant to him. She listened to him, she heard him, she knew him, and she made him feel safe, and grounded, and complete. Her name is Barb, and they shared a lot of special times together. He tells me all the time how sad he was when they lost touch after their last conversation with each other in 1972. She was very special to him, more than she knew, and always will be.

I am going to jump to Steve now for a bit. He is also a very old soul and very special to me, like Jim is. Steve is a year older than Jim; they are Irish twins. They are very close, with a special bond from this life and all previous lives they have had together. They have been brothers many times. They will be brothers again in their next lives, for which they are already making plans – and I *love that!*

Steve was active in sports, and he loved cars. He had an El Camino that he loved and cherished with all his heart. Even though he may have been a bit rough and tough on it, as boys can be, he still babied that car. Steve also loved working with his hands. He was creative and talented and loved creating things like windchimes. That was his safe place to relax and be himself.

He also loved Christmas. Every year since they have been with me, they both sit and look at my tree, its lights and the decorations, and have a beer. Steve will also have a can of original Pringles to enjoy in these calm, soothing times. This is when they look the most relaxed and happy. As I write this, they are saying *"Good memories, good memories."*

Steve was fond of Aerosmith, Pink Floyd, and ZZ Top. I never knew him in this lifetime either, but I do know they only lived about twenty minutes from where I grew up and where I live now. It sure is a small world.

One night, Jim and Steve wanted to connect with me. They started the conversation with *"Back in the day, when things were simpler and free, and that 1972 was a GREAT YEAR!"* They were sharing with me a vision of a lot of lemons in the kitchen. They said I *had* to put this in as this is a memory that was very important, and that if someone from their past were to read this book, they would know who they were and remember the good times they had together.

They started to talk about a local area named Valley Falls located in Vernon, Connecticut, where they would go in their cars and hang out and listen to loud music with their buddies/chums and many girls and just party. OMG – the old cars they talked about! They described an orange Gremlin. It was an odd shape and had a hatchback. They talked about a 1972 black Dodge, and a black Corvette that was creepy to them because there were crime-related incidents that took place in that car.

They said the Corvette belonged to their creepy neighbor that lived down the road from them in Tolland. His name is Vito. They showed me another car, but just the inside. It had a red interior and steering wheel. They were *not* in this car, as it was creepy beyond words to them.

Steve loved his El Camino. He had a feather roach clip hanging from the rearview mirror, and he played loud music in it. This car had a much better vibe to it than the Corvette did.

Even though Jim and Steve feel that 1972 was a great year with all the dancing and loud music, all the girls and parties, and they were carefree, they were also very cautious because of what they were going through and what they knew. Steve started to fear for his life in 1968 when he experienced for the first time a crime that his brother Devin committed in front of him. What they were going to endure in the future terrified them to the bone. This would lead to their premature deaths.

They carry so much pain and guilt from their family secrets and what the town of Tolland, Connecticut held and still holds to this day. Family and blood are *not* always the best people to be around as some can be more toxic than the devil. Trust, honesty, and security was replaced with dishonesty, lies, deception, and crime of all kinds – and massive torture. Jim never got the chance to graduate from high school, get married, and have a family of his own in the traditional, loving way he would have liked. He never got to experience any of the future bands that he would have loved to listen to and could relate to. He never got his band on the charts or made his dreams and goals a reality.

Jim's life was cut short due to other people's sick, demented actions. He was threatened to stay quiet and filled with more guilt each day, hour, and minute from the things he was forced to know about and do, for fear of his life. He was made to keep quiet by their older brother Devin, and by creepy neighbors such as Vito, as well as their fathers, who thrived on and still thrive on destroying others daily even today.

As Jim endured this guilt, pain, and torture daily, one October day in 1974, he decided to skip school and go back home and be with himself and his thoughts. He was interested in doing some drugs as well just to relax himself. When he entered his home, he found that Devin was also there. They engaged in a conversation that resulted Devin giving Jim pill and liquid form drugs. Jim became disoriented; nothing made sense. The feeling he felt was nothing like he felt before. Devin held a gun to his head, moved it to his neck, then to his heart, and then to the back left side of his head. Devin took Jim's hand and placed it on the gun and Devin made Jim's hand pull the trigger. Jim looked at his hand and saw the blood. He also turned around in a nearby mirror and saw the blood dripping from his head and said, "I have been shot." The ambulance came and he later passed away in a nearby hospital. Jim has told me numerous times that he was foolish for skipping school that day and definitely not proud of that action, but back then that's what kids did.

He wasn't the only one who had skipped school that day, there was a young girl that did as well from the middle school, and she traveled through the grassy areas in a fast pace in fear she would be caught. As she did, she witnessed some of what happened and never spoke of it. When you witness something as bad as this, it's always best to speak the truth even if you knew the person or not. These people should have done the right thing.

Jim would no longer hear music physically, would never make people laugh again, or even graduate high school, or see and speak to Barb as he had hoped. He was only 17 years old. This breaks my heart, and it makes me extremely angry and sick to my stomach that this beautiful soul had to leave this earth because of the evil being done by a family member and by the community he lived in, as they have kept quiet for many decades to come. Was this suicide? Or was this murder? Per Jim, it was murder, as he would never, ever attempt suicide.

When Jim died, Steve was beyond devastated, as they were very close, to say the least. They were and are soulmates. He remained devastated for many years to come. He kept a shirt of Jim's, to have a piece of him forever. He tried to be happy, but he missed Jim too much. His old soul became a lost soul.

Steve had an even rougher life after Jim died. It was hard for him to move on. He didn't have the best of luck, and things spiraled out of control as he was filled with guilt and pain, while being tortured to keep quiet with what he, too, was forced to know and do. He tried his best, but it just got to be too much. He started to self-medicate to try to ease the pain, but nothing would work. He never told people what he endured, even the ones he thought he could be close to. He buried the truth deep down inside himself to never be mentioned again. Both boys tried going to the police and other adults such as teachers, but they were both ignored repeatedly.

Steve was, in a way, luckier than Jim. He did get married and had two daughters. He would love to redo that time with his children and have them know the truth and have them see that their dad was a wonderful innocent man and let them know how much he loved and still loves them with everything he has. He wanted to see his two beautiful daughters grow up and have children of their own in the traditional way, but due to the disturbing actions of others, he was unable to. Like Jim, his death was made to look like a suicide, but it wasn't. It was murder. Steve would not have attempted suicide either. They had both thought about it at times but could never follow through. It just wasn't who they were. They were also not evil beings. They were full of love and couldn't hurt themselves or anyone else on purpose.

On a frigid cold day in February in 1998, Steve was beaten up badly a few times before he was hung up in a tree. The torture didn't end when he was hanged even though he was already dead when Devin hung him. Devin continued to kick and swing Steve and beat his face to where his eyes hung out from his beautiful face. There was a female bystander watching and hoping to gain a handful of cash for luring Steve to this area, but she never got a dime. She did get to say goodbye to Steve with a few slaps on his face and spitting on him.

After the brutal beating and hanging, another male came to this area which is behind where the Big Y in Tolland, CT, is today. He wanted to make sure the job was done. This man had new Italian orange brown dress shoes that were just freshly polished and was very well dressed. He told Devin he had done a great job, but it needed one final last touch. Devin took a knife and made three slices in Steve's heart. They stood proudly, looking at the work they just completed and this male that was well dressed said now the job is done. This man was Vito, the neighbor down the street from where they lived. Steve was 41 years old.

Steve never, ever talked about his own death with me, until recently. He started slowly showing me what happened, and I mean very slowly. It was devastating for him to show me; even Jim had to step in many times to finish sharing the information. The boys had to take many breaks when they started to tell me. When they saw how angry, frustrated, and disgusted I was getting, I saw how embarrassed, frightened and angry they were. I decided to put it in this book now as it needs to be told, but there will be more information about this and many other hidden secrets that will surface as well in the next book as there are many layers to this story and everything will be coming out and the truth will be known to the world.

Steve was stronger than Jim – not that Jim was weak, because he certainly wasn't. Everyone's experiences are different. Steve tried to change things, but he couldn't for fear of his life and of those of others he was close to such as his two daughters, not to mention the exhaustion he felt. Those boys – and I call them boys because that is how they show themselves to me; this is when they were at their happiest on this earth –are both equally beautiful loving souls with huge hearts. I visit their graves in Rhode Island. It brings much peace to me. I clean up the gravestones when they are covered with grass as this cemetery is not well taken care of. They ask when I go, to bring a red rose for their mom and blue flowers for them. It's the least I can do to try and bring some peace to their final resting place.

Some who knew them may say differently about their personalities, as things were different in the 1970s. It was a different time, when families were brought up in a different way. Laws and rules were very different. Power and money had a way of speaking loudly, as it still does today, and it had control over some people. You didn't step on anyone's toes or overstep, or even question others then – not even your parents.

Both boys were known for their knowledge and talents, silly antics, and brotherly love. They were very smart, and it showed, but at the same time it backfired. They also were known as the local bad boys in Tolland, Connecticut and surrounding towns due to the reputation of their older brother Devin and many others with their demented minds and actions.

If everyone had worked together back then, things would have and could have turned out differently. These boys would still be here. Steve enjoying his two girls and Jim making it big in the music industry. But thanks to the cowardly and greedy actions of other people, namely teachers and local law enforcement, town officials, local fire departments, and innocent bystanders that chose to keep quiet about the things that were happening at that time, 50-plus years of pain and unanswered questions have gone by for many, many families and innocent victims. These boys never had a chance but the kept fighting as long as they could.

When one doesn't listen to someone who is speaking and instead chooses to ignore the information they are hearing, it results in more pain and suffering, and even the unnecessary deaths of more innocent people.

I also want to share how Jim and Steve helped me trust and move ahead in my journey. They really know me better than I know myself at times. They make the lessons challenging yet doable. Life is never easy, and I learned it is not supposed to be. We are learning every day. I have come a very long way since I met these two.

As I mentioned earlier, I was working at a local CVS. I truly loved it there, and the people I worked with. But with my gifts advancing at a rapid pace, I had to focus on my true purpose on this earth, and that was helping people by bringing peace, clarity, and healing energy to others for the Lord.

It was a very, very hard decision to leave my retail job. It took me about four months to decide, because I needed to work and support myself for a while longer.

The boys told me it was time to leave that job and start reading full time. They taught me to trust and believe in myself and them and, of course, I did. I made my decision to leave the store when it was getting to be too exhausting and just too much.

I am truly blessed to have had that job and the opportunity to grow in many directions and learn more about myself. When I did leave, it was bittersweet.

I still keep in contact with some of my friends from there. They are part of my support team, and they will *never* lead me in the wrong direction.

Now, I was doing readings on two online psychic reading sites, Lifereader.com and Keen.com. I put all my energy into those sites as well as my own business, Hearing from Heaven.

While doing all this, I was working on all the information they were giving me about their lives as well, so I was pretty busy, and loved every minute of it. But I never put my boys over my family. I somehow balanced all this with my family obligations.

I found that I had been bringing peace and healing to others more and more by the reviews I received from my clients. This is how I knew I made the right choice. I knew I had grown a lot spiritually thanks to the reviews I was receiving from my clients after a few years of doing readings. I will share some of them below with you, as I did in Chapter 4 with the reviews from when I was first getting started.

These reviews gave me a lot of confidence to keep going and to trust my intuition no matter where it is going to lead me. I am here to fulfill my purpose that the Lord has chosen me to do.

Reviews After I Went Full Time with My Readings

WOW! Mind-blowing! In tune with your emotions and with all that is going on within you. She's excellent!

Highly recommend reading with her. Thank you so much!

It was wonderful and very spot on, thank you! I will definitely be a continuing client when I purchase another reading. She is very sweet and helpful! I can't thank you enough for your help.

I absolutely adore this advisor!! She is ALWAYS on point with everything, I mean everything... She is my top go-to advisor. Thank you so, so much.

She's so doggone SPOT-ON!!!! Yesssssss.

Whatever you read in these comments, they are all true. She knows exactly what is happening to you and what message you need to receive. She is great!

Genuinely one of best readers on here, second time with her and again very accurate with little information from my side - no sugar coating but kind.

I ran out of funds, but this reading was amazing. I'm blown away and never had a reading like this before!!I appreciate you!

Another great reading with Momma! She's been right about everything! She picked up on my POI and his fears, she even picked up how my kids have been feeling, and I never once mentioned having kids! More than 5 stars!! Plus talking to her is like chatting with a best friend!

She is amazing! So spot-on about everything literally. Will definitely reach out to her again!

This woman has always been spot-on and her intuition and sense towards people has been right. I always come back to ask what her guidance is.

SO SO amazing, please don't hesitate to pick her. She confirmed everything! without much info. Talking to her was also easy, with no judgment, like a good friend. I wanted to cry, and she didn't tell me what I wanted to hear either. very honest yet compassionate

You are the best! After our chat this morning my poi texted me twice today!!! You even knew why I was chatting with you without me saying anything!!! I'm so happy and always grateful for our chats... don't get tired of them please, Lol.

She is absolutely amazing. The way that she delivers the truth you seek is so helpful. And she sees it all.

Very impressed. Knew exactly what was going on without any details or hints that could lead her to any conclusions. Simply amazed. Very helpful and reassuring. Will be back.

Amazing reading. Very thoughtful, using the right words and explaining everything. Very empathic, feels like you are talking to a friend or sibling. I recommend 1000%.

Yes, yes ,yes and yes 🖤🕊️ the best!!!

Giftedmomma0911 is an absolute joy to chat with. It is hard to stop! She is very compassionate, kind, and gifted. She has helped me tremendously. Don't hesitate to reach out!

This woman is by far one of the most gifted people on the platform. They knew things I never mentioned from the beginning of the reading and continued to know things I had never said. Thank you so much for everything.

Omg, completely blown away!!! Thank you so much love!

Thank you! She is the absolute best reader on Keen. com.

Chatting with my clients is like talking to a friend. I am happy for their success and feel very proud of them as they grow and learn their lessons in each of their individual journeys.

You cannot compare one journey to another. We are all unique beings. That is what makes the balance here on earth. What I really enjoy and love is when my clients call me by my screen name, which is Giftedmomma0911. They call me gifted, momma, and GM-gifted momma. That shows me that we have a strong bond, and that, to me, is very important, as my mission is to bring peace and clarity to others. I never judge others.

The boys have taught me a lot. They have brought me out of my comfort zone, as you know, and taught me to trust myself and to be my own go-to person rather than to rely on others. You must stand up for yourself, provide for yourself, help others, and believe, believe, and believe in yourself.

They got me through everything I needed to get through at that time when I was on my own and was learning all this, and they continue to do so. I still have many challenges, as we all do. That is life. That's what keeps us going and moving forward and makes us stronger. I have learned a lot about myself, and I now see the pattern of my life as to why things have happened and when, and why things haven't happened.

There is no one way to go; there are *always* options in every situation. Not everyone is the same. We all learn differently, we don't express ourselves the same, our paths are not the same. Narrow-minded thinking does not work. You must be *open-minded*. There, you will find all the options and a whole new world.

For example, the traditional way of going to school, starting with preschool or kindergarten going up to twelfth grade then graduating is not for everyone. Not everyone learns that way. There are different ways that you can go about getting a diploma and different environments you can use to do it. We need to open our minds and look past the standard way of operating. With my journey, I know for a fact *everything is possible!*

Working with my boys has certainly been an adventure. Again, if I wasn't going through this, I would never believe it myself. Everything I'm telling you in this book is 100% the full truth. There are no coincidences. There is so much more to this one planet Earth, the universe, heaven, and hell. All of it is real; people are just oblivious to their surroundings because their fear takes over.

I will no longer question what happens. Instead, I will find out why it happened or didn't happen, and I will do this with my boys, Jim and Steve, as I trust them with my life, and with guidance and direction as to where I am supposed to go and where they are to lead me. This brings me to why this chapter is about *getting to know My Boys*. They trust me as well with their lives, their afterlives, and their stories, and they chose me to help them be heard so they can have freedom and peace in heaven, because they left this planet way too soon, under many others' thumbs and deception.

It is extremely important to me to get their stories out to the public and have them known, because it affects many, many people and families. *Tolland County, Connecticut needs answers!*

Jim and Steve have chosen me to be their voice to bring peace and freedom to them and others, both living and dead. I am honored to tell their stories, and I will *not* let them down. I will do this with or without the proper authorities. I will bulldoze through this until it surfaces, and the whole truth is out, and the people that are still alive who caused all of this are put behind bars.

CHAPTER 7

LIVING, LOVING, AND LAUGHING WITH "MY BOYS"

Jim and Steve would often play Pink Floyd's song "Wish You Were Here" on the car radio, as they send spiritual messages to me this way. The part about the two lost souls with the same old fears suits them to a T.

Oh... My Boys! This is *exactly* how they feel: just going around and around and around wondering what to do and looking at all the same pain in others here on earth that they both endured in their lifetime as well. This includes the innocent victims of all ages, their families, their friends, their community, and others' communities in the surrounding towns. My Boys have also been looking at the people that have caused all this pain and continue to cause it to this day.

They tried to stop what was happening but ran out of strength as the pain and torture grew. Family and blood are *not always* the best to be around as they tend to wreak more havoc and take control of what is *not* theirs. Again, when people choose to ignore the signs and evidence of what others are saying, nothing good can come of it, whether it's parents, family, friends, neighbors, teachers, or law enforcement and the community – *yes* – *law enforcement, teachers, and the community*. I write this with a heavy heart, as none of these acts should have happened. They could have been prevented, but weren't due to cruelty, power, money, and the actions and inactions of others; it was not stopped.

In this chapter, however, I would like to share some of the funny moments the boys and I have had. They asked me to add this in so they can smile again. It makes them feel complete that someone is listening and helping them – *finally!* – and that they are helping me and others too.

It's truly amazing how they can communicate from heaven. They can really move energy. The times we have together keep us all going. They can be hysterical, mischievous, stunning, serious, and so down-to-earth – no pun intended. They have the biggest hearts, the most loving and caring energy, and I love how protective they are of me.

They have had too much sadness in their lives, and I would like to share with you what makes them feel good and happy, and how they help me and others from where they are now in heaven. They are really two beautiful souls, and they deserve recognition for all the work and effort they have made here on earth and in heaven to get the truth out so justice can be served.

Living with My Boys, what can I say? Other than it sure has been a wild ride. It was nothing I would ever have thought I would or could experience. I was always intrigued by the paranormal stories in books and on television. Although everyone has experienced spiritual happenings in their lives, I feel I have experienced more than others on a massively high level. I can no longer watch those kinds of shows, as I have seen a lot with the visions I have been shown. I will be sharing with you some of the experiences I have had with Jim and Steve. The things these boys can do really makes my jaw drop.

In my eyes, there is nothing they can't do.

How the Boys Have Helped Me and Made/Make Me Laugh

When we first started communicating, they would literally wake me up in the middle of the night and want to write. I kept a notebook and pen on my bed. This happened in the middle of the night because it is easier at that time to cross between heaven and earth, as that is when the layers are thinner. They would literally put the pen in my hand and my glasses on. I could feel it all. I had never heard of this in my life. It's wild.

We would write for a long time. They would give me information on many different things, and warnings as to what to check for if someone was doing something behind my back. I would check these things out, and sure enough, they were spot-on with all they had written.

Jim loves to use his handprints as a sign he is here and near. They are never too far from me. Again, that's how they surround, escort, and protect me. I was alone, and as I knew how everything around me was laid out and could be always located and in detail, if someone moved or changed something, I would notice it quickly. I love walking around the house and finding handprints from them. It's so cool how they can do that.

Jim also loves to draw pictures on the carpet. He got to know my daytime habits, so he knew where I was going to walk. Just traveling around the house as I worked and went about my days, I would suddenly see pictures that he had drawn on the carpet to get my attention. He drew a map and a picture of a teacher. Again, I had never heard of this. It was just mind blowing!!

Jim *never* had the chance to experience things such as cell phones and computers because he died in 1974, and these things were not available until much later. Since we have been hanging out, he loves touching my computer. I will be sitting and working on my laptop, and when I take breaks for lunch or a walk, I will come back and find that my laptop has a message or a picture that he would want me to look at. The same thing with my phone. He will freeze my screens if he doesn't want me to send something to someone. I get the hints. Again, it is mind-blowing!

Both Jim and Steve love cats and dogs, and I find it hilarious when our dog plays with the boys. It's hysterical to watch as my dog stands in front of the kitchen but won't go in and starts barking and wagging his tail. Another funny interaction happens when one of them is sitting on the couch. My dog jumps to the spot in front of where they are sitting on the couch, then backs up and barks and wags his tail and repeats this four times. He gets so excited to play. There are times when we are out walking, and Steve will show up about 100 feet ahead of us. The dog will suddenly stop and stare ahead, so I will look and see Steve there. Then the dog barks and wags his tail. It's so nice to see the boys smile and still enjoy something they loved when they were alive.

These guys love to mess with me. They play jokes on me, and I know it's them because they start to laugh afterwards. One night, we were all walking around the block. We were about three houses away from home, and suddenly, I felt the pressure of my legs and body being dragged backwards, like Michael Jackson's moonwalk. I was like, "Okay now, you two goons cool it." Then they started to laugh, and I felt a swirl of breezes around me. Very cool!

They are always on me to stay active and eat right, so they are with me on my walks and hikes. One morning, I was on a walk with the dog. About halfway through the walk, I hear laughing behind us, so I look back and see nothing there. I look ahead again, and I see three shadows on the road in front of me: mine, the dog's, and Steve's. I had to count who was there to make sure it was just the dog and me, because there were three shadows.

Another time on our nightly walk, there were cars in front of the dog and me, parked on the side of the road. We were coming up behind the car, which was on a slight hill, and I heard *"Move over."* So, I did. I heard it again *"Move over, Susan,"* so I did again. Well, I guess I didn't move far enough so they literally picked my body up and put me on the grass. As soon as I was set down, there was a car coming fast the other way. If I had walked past that parked car on that slight hill, I would have been hit. This is part of their practice of carefully protecting me that I keep talking about.

Jim and Steve have helped me in so many ways that it would take a lifetime to tell everything. They think they are funny when they shake my bed at night to wake me up. I'm like, "Okay now, okay, I will write!"

They have helped my gifts open and advance. They protect me while I am doing readings. I love it when they bang on the walls and make noises and cause a ruckus, just like brothers do with each other. It makes me so happy to see them happy and laughing and smiling. They deserve to be happy, as they were robbed of this in their life on Earth. The other thing they have done is to tell me when to take a video on my phone. I will do this and see orbs - colorful ones - and I can see them walking and sitting, and I can hear them talking when I go back and review the videos.

Jim and Steve have not only helped me, but when I ask them to help my two closest friends, one in England and one in Ohio, they are right there to help. This warms my heart. They really help them with whatever they are going through at the time.

I want to share one other very cool act that Steve did. I was outside one day and saw him standing in front of me. I smiled. He started to point in a direction for me to turn and look. I followed his direction and walked with him. He stopped and pointed down, so I looked down. I don't know how this could happen, but it did. I saw his last name written in paint for me to see. I was flabbergasted beyond words.

They also love to meditate with me. They are so amazing in meditation. They know when to come forth, when to stand aside, and when to act. They love moving my head and neck to relax. I love seeing them on their knees when the Lord Jesus comes.

They are so respectful. They also protect me when other spirits want to communicate with me. There was one male that had wanted to connect, and I did NOT like the energy or feel comfortable talking with this male. His energy made me so sick and weak that I had to leave my retail job one night. They said it was their father. I said I couldn't talk with him right then. They respected my boundaries. It took me about a year before I was ready to talk to him. Again, these boys are always with me on many different levels.

We laugh, cry, scream, and express anger and sadness together. I understand them and they understand me. I accept them and they accept me. We do not judge each other in any way, shape, or form. There are no secrets - that's for sure. They see and hear everything. But I don't mind. I treasure having them in my life, and I wouldn't have it any other way.

CHAPTER 8

ACCEPTING AND LIVING WITH MY ABILITIES

As I mentioned earlier, I have *always* been intrigued and obsessed by paranormal activities – death, cemeteries, bones, dead bodies, the afterlife, and funeral homes... but only behind the scenes. I do *not* like to attend funerals. I always must know what was going to happen and how it was in the past. I can *never* stay in the present.

This was a massive challenge for me. I couldn't understand any of this. The day I found out I was a psychic medium, I was thrilled, excited, and simply beside myself. I had finally found the reason as to why I am here on this earth. I knew I had to keep moving forward and learn and understand what I had to do and why I was given these special gifts by the Lord.

I started slowly as I was a stay-at-home mom at the time, so I needed to use my own time wisely. I started to read up on psychics and mediums, and learned that I was lucky to be both, and very grateful that I was literally working for the Lord himself as he is the one that has given me my gifts. After the excitement wore off, I became a bit more grounded and focused. I had to accept all this, and I wasn't sure where to start.

I had to learn everything through experiences and guidance. I have always been a one-on-one, visual learner. So, I had to find a way to do this on my own. I thought, *Okay, as we all have lessons in life to learn, this is one of mine.* I learned to trust my instincts and myself along with what I was seeing, hearing, and feeling.

Clairvoyance (seeing) and Claircognizance (knowing) were the first two tools to develop for my intuition tool bag. At first, it was hard to trust what I was seeing and hearing and knowing. Was it real or was it something I put in my head myself?

Being an empath is the same, as you pick up others' emotions no matter what they are. You must decipher what is yours and what is not, what is real and what is not. For a beginner this is very hard to do. Once I started to decipher these things, it started to make sense. Then it snowballed for me, and I know what is mine and what is not.

When my abilities first started to open, it was the negative vibes that came out first. Then it moved to the happier things and became a mix of the two. I was so excited to have this cool intuition, but what you see, hear, know, and feel is not always pleasant.

I had always said I wanted to have this intuition all the time, but be careful what you wish for, because with me, it never shuts off. I feel this is why it's hard for me to be in the present, as I have so many levels to pay attention to. I had to learn to accept this and remind myself once again that everything in life includes the good and the bad. This is what makes the balance of things and the world go around.

I started to learn how to meditate. This was not easy, as I found it hard to sit still and quiet my mind as there is always something running through it. I started with just a few minutes a day. I didn't feel like I was doing anything, but over time it started to connect for me, and I stuck with it. Today, I do it daily.

The information that starts to come through is beyond amazing, whether it is personal or work related. I enjoy all the messages and loved ones that come through. It's like my psychic writing, but visual, and it helps with so much more. It clears negative energy, clears chakras, brings in positive energy, and balances and grounds me. I know I must stick with this as it's part of my job, and if I am working for the Lord, I need to have all the right tools in my intuition bag.

Another tool that I find that helps me is breathworks. The breathworks technique is used to release toxins and stress when you breathe out, and to nourish your mind and body when you breathe in. This feels so refreshing and relaxing and is one of my favorites.

It took me a while to get used to all these new ways of living. I had to accept what I had been given, and once I did that, things started to slowly fall into place. As with anything we need to learn, it takes time. I found these tools by trusting my instincts and what I was hearing and seeing.

The boys are fond of these tools as well. The visions I was getting from the boys showed me what to do and where to go to learn about these tools. In my visions, I would see words literally being written and spelled out and formed into a sentence – so very cool! I would Google what I saw and, sure enough, I would find out about what I had been told. I was where I was supposed to be. Doing this helped me accept that I was not crazy and that what I was experiencing was all real and the start of the new me.

I was on my own for a while, learning and accepting and loving every minute of what I was able to do. I started to incorporate all of this into my daily life. I started to see more of the path of my journey, and how it was unfolding – slowly, which is fine with me. I am here to help others by relaying messages from passed loved ones, and the Lord himself along with Archangel Michael and others to help with direction and guidance.

The Lord and Archangel Michael also enter my readings when needed. Again, this is all about teamwork and getting the result to the client that is needed at the time. The boys will also let me know when to back off or stop in a reading if I need to, to protect myself when a reading is getting way too deep and entering a bad territory.

By this time, I was gaining more self-confidence and self-esteem. I was going out of my comfort zone and trying to learn more and trying different things. As each psychic medium uses their own set of tools and develops their own style, I realized I had to do the same thing. I always thought all psychic mediums *had* to do palm readings and use tarot cards, crystals, and crystal balls, or had to be face-to-face for readings.

Well, I found out that is *not* true. As I tried different things such as essential oils, crystals, tarot cards, oracle cards, and more, I found what worked for me. I listened to the direction I was receiving, trusted that direction and guidance as it was coming into me and went with it rather than questioning it. As I was drawn to certain things and not drawn to others, I found more of my tools and the subjects that I would be working on with my clients. I listed these in Chapter Two.

I am extremely happy and grateful for what I am helping others with. I also started to notice a pattern in my readings, such as the psychic typing, and Archangel Michael and the Lord himself coming into my readings. The subjects were like the life lessons I have been through myself. I must relate to the issue to help others get through it. This is all part of life's journey. It's funny how life turns out and works out. I learned not to question things anymore but to go with the flow of things and accept what is and what isn't.

I have learned so much about myself with this journey I am on. I have learned self-love and self-care and to accept myself for who I am. I have made many changes in my life that were not easy to make, but all my lessons brought me through some challenging times and made me stronger. I realized that until I saw and accepted each challenge, it wasn't going to go away. I had to make changes. Changes are growth. Growth is moving ahead and living, and living is what we are supposed to be doing.

One of the things I had to get used to, again slowly, was the length of readings I offered through Hearing from Heaven. Tuning into others and their loved ones as well really takes a lot of energy out of me. I had to pace myself, as it would exhaust me. As I offered longer readings with online chats with Hearing from Heaven on Facebook, I developed the experience of handling the long chats for when I went to Lifereader. com and Keen.com. Slow and steady was good for me.

I tried face-to-face readings and did readings at a local coffee shop in Windsor, Connecticut. It went well, but I had to accept that face-to-face is not for me. I find chats are more my style. I can concentrate more on getting my client the answers that are needed for them to move forward in their journey while I work in privacy from the comfort of my own home.

The one part of this journey that has been very hard for me to accept is that the Lord himself has told me *several times*, and even my psychic medium sisters as well, that I am a *very rare psychic medium* and that I am one of a handful of us on this planet.

No other psychic medium has a relationship with their guides like I do with my guides, *My Boys - Jim and Steve*. They have even told me this same thing many times. I feel very grateful and privileged. But yet again, why me? Why am I to be one of the rare ones? Why did Jim, Steve, and Sweetpea come to me for help? Why me? Why me? Why me? (I will tell you more about Sweetpea in later chapters.)

I find it extremely difficult and lonely being a *rare one*. I find that no one really understands me and what I went through to have been given these gifts. Within the past year, my healing hands have been developing - another amazing gift from the Lord. I can help my clients with anxiety and lower their heart rates back to normal. I can help with pain management, PMS, migraines, and much more.

Again, why me? I find myself very lonely and misunderstood. The word *jealousy* has come up a *lot*, and I just can't believe people would be jealous of me. It comes up so much at times that I just want to isolate myself, but then I think, *NO, this is my journey*. It's a lot of pressure at times, too. But I turn that around and when there is jealousy around me, I use it as motivation to move forwards. I had to cut ties with others because of this as they would become negative energy for me. I have set many boundaries to protect my energy. I have had other psychics and friends and family members send bad vibes my way due to their jealousy. That is not cool. That is *NOT* teamwork. Hurting people and wishing bad on them on purpose is never a good option. It will always catch up to you, not to mention I can see who it is and send it back.

I had to learn how to protect myself and I have learned not to let my guard down and to set boundaries as bad can come through anywhere and everywhere. Cleansing and grounding myself is extremely beneficial on many levels and an absolute must. I will cleanse and ground myself and I will also from time to time have my psychic friend do a scan and an overall cleanse. Remember, there are no secrets, and everything does come out. It's just a matter of time.

There is nothing better and more satisfying than living your true purpose, doing your part to make the balance in this world. We should all be doing that, because then the world would be a better place, a better world, a more loving and caring and giving world. People would be much happier as they would have done their true best with no regrets or guilt. You would be able to put your head down on your pillow at night knowing you did your best, and that is a great feeling.

Life is learning, accepting, and forgiving yourself so you can move ahead to accomplish the purpose(s) for why you are here, as this makes the path in our journey easier to travel. *If you choose not to listen and choose to ignore all the signs you are given, you will not move ahead and you will be stuck and stay there.* You will not accomplish your true purpose and you will have many regrets and much guilt, not to mention unbalancing the world.

Some people will have what they chose to ignore eat them alive as they grow older. Later, as you stay stuck, or in some cases can move ahead and live your life while pretending things didn't happen and choosing to keep quiet, it's only a matter of time before Miss Karma comes knocking at your door. Whether it's months after or 50 years later, you will eventually need to face your maker.

That choice you made will have affected many, many innocent people for years to come. It's best, instead, to use teamwork and do the right thing. The result may not always be pleasant, but it will be the right thing to do rather than being a coward and living a fake life.

Again, when people abandon teamwork and try to express themselves in every way shape and form that they can, and others – *especially teachers and law enforcement* – choose not to listen, or hurt people on purpose, it is an abuse of their authority. More people get hurt as their lives are torturous and full of fear, including fear of their lives being taken. Then they can't find anyone to listen, or trust anyone enough to listen, not even their own family.

Sometimes, your own flesh and blood or loved ones can be part of the problem. Again, this results in having many, many innocent people affected by that one choice that could have prevented all the pain that was caused for many years to follow.

It has been almost six years now that I have been receiving information on local cold cases and more, and I will tell you the line of people that were involved, and are involved still to this day, whether doing the crime itself or staying quiet. It is unfathomable. It goes so deep. All towns have their secrets, but in my opinion Tolland County has been number one on the charts from what I have seen and heard from my boys they were there going through it. There is so much information and many levels of deep secrets and pain. There will need to be a whole other book to tell more of what the boys have shared with me.

CHAPTER 9

PREPARING TO WORK WITH JIM AND STEVE

This is one of my favorite sayings. I just absolutely fell in love with it. I took this photograph myself and saved it to use in this book.

The one thing that I found when I started to focus on my intuition is that I had to slow down and listen.

I had no choice but to listen so I would know what everyone was saying to me and showing me. It was always hard for me to stay still long enough for anything physically and mentally, for things like concerts, plays, weddings, any kind of large event, even a manicure. It was a *massive* challenge for me.

The boys taught me how to slow down and be patient, and how to listen to my soul, to follow my instincts, and to trust and believe in myself. The way they have shown me things and explained things was in baby steps so I could put the puzzle pieces together and see the full picture. One way they have shown me to slow down and be patient was by writing with them.

Jim loves to write, as that was part of him when he was here. There were no computers (it was the 1970s), so he never experienced them. The traditional, old-school, pen-and-paper way of communicating was how he got me to slow down. Connecting like this meant I would have to sit quietly and focus so he could write.

Steve is different. He loves to write as well, but he will also psychically auto type with me. They both prefer writing, as it is quality time for all three of us together, and other souls that I have written with as well.

These guys have a tremendous amount of patience with me. I sometimes wonder who has the harder job, me or them. Again, when it's teamwork, it doesn't matter as all the participants have a job to do.

This chapter is going to be about how the boys and I started to work together. The connection we have is truly amazing. They really know me, and I really know them. When I get stuck in my life, they are the ones I turn to, along with my parents, and they will always answer and comfort me, and direct and guide me in ways no one else could ever do on a spiritual level.

The four main things the boys wanted me to focus on were meditation, deep breathing, writing/auto typing, and my dreams. These are their favorites, and they can get their information to me much easier with these techniques, as the information flows smoothly this way. So, this is our foundation. We use these techniques daily.

This was very different and new to me, but they knew how to get their messages across to me. Another technique the boys push for me is exercise and health. They are always on my butt to stay healthy and to walk. My health is extremely good, but I have a few pounds to lose, so they tell me to walk, walk, walk. They love to go hiking with me, and they can get silly, cheering me on as I go up hills.

As we continue to write/type, meditate, and deep-breathe together, our bond with each other gets stronger and stronger. They have told me many times over that our connection and relationship is like no other between other psychic mediums and their guides. It is unheard of. As I go through this journey of mine, I totally believe that, as I can feel it. I can't explain it, but I must agree with them.

As Jim and Steve continued to teach me how to use my intuition and accept it and live with it, it became much easier. They took baby steps, as they knew things would overwhelm me when they would start to tell me their story. It compares to taking one step at a time instead of climbing an entire staircase at once. It works so much better, and you can appreciate the journey more as you are seeing all of it.

Another technique they introduced me to and knew would help me is meditation with Mother Earth. This is so amazing! I have had many experiences with this.

I have also had Mother Teresa come through, and she offered her hand to help heal me in a time of need.

The Lord himself comes in quite often. He offers his hands and love and tells me what I need to hear, not just what I want to hear. He reassures me that I am here to work for him by helping others. When he speaks, of course I *must* listen. He also reassures me that I am on the right path and thanks me for my work.

The boys and I have created a routine to practice our techniques daily. It's all part of my work. Just like a doctor continues to learn about medicine as part of their work. Athletes need to work out. We are always growing and learning and advancing. I always wanted to know why I was here, and now I do. I have been shown my path, my journey.

They have taught me and will continue to teach me what I need to know to do my job. They have also shown me how to trust myself and my instinct. They have also shown me how to use fear to rise and not run. For everything they have done for me, I am proud to be their anchor and voice to this earth, to tell their story, and get peace for them.

There is *nothing* in this world I will not do for them. I respect and support these two boys with all my heart and soul, and I always will. I know these boys are innocent. When it's my time to go to heaven, they will be there at the door to welcome me with open arms, and I am fully sure with some silly antics.

They have never let me down or given me wrong information. It may not be what I want to hear at times, but I accept what they tell and show me. Then I see why something didn't happen or why it did happen, depending on what it was.

What I didn't know yet, as they started to prepare me to receive their information via visions, audio, writing, and more, was that I couldn't have been prepared enough as to how sad and devastating their stories truly are.

The amazing thing about these beautiful souls everywhere is that they can speak from the grave and tell the truth of things, as there are always two sides to every story.

I found out that Jim and Steve were kids living in Tolland, Connecticut, and that their older brother was murdering people of all ages and committing all sorts of crimes.

These boys need to tell the story, along with Sweetpea's.

CHAPTER 10

GETTING TO KNOW
"MY SWEETPEA"

I must say that this journey of mine has really been remarkable. If I had not seen and experienced it myself, I would not believe it. I have learned so much, from growing up, to adulthood, to meeting Jim and Steve – and Sweetpea. I have grown so much spiritually and have seen and felt so much over the first few years of getting to know my abilities and practicing them and coming out of my comfort zone. It brings me great joy to bring peace, clarity, and guidance and direction to others. This is my passion, and I will do this for the rest of my life – or as long as I am called to do it.

I consider myself extremely lucky and grateful for watching and understanding my life's path unfold. I feel that not everyone is able to see or understand that, so they remain lost and question what their purpose truly is. Life is never easy, and it wasn't meant to be. We are not here to sit and wait for things to be handed to us. We need to meet the universe at least halfway by doing the legwork here while the universe is working on its part up there for us. We are all here for a purpose, to do our part to make this world go around.

To make this world go around, it needs balance, as with everything in life, whether it's happy and sad, love and hate, admiration and jealousy, black and white, good and evil, crime and passion, theft and murder, power and death. No matter what it is, that balance must be there; unfortunately, even if it's right and wrong.

I have come to accept and enjoy my intuition and my journey. It's not perfect by any means, as nothing in the world is, but it's mine and I understand it and I will treasure each day and stop and smell every flower on the way. The key is to accept the good with the bad.

When my visions first started, I thought, *WOW, what is this?* As they became clearer and more vivid, it was like watching a movie in my head. I didn't know the people or the places, but what I was being shown felt familiar. So I went with my intuition, and instead of questioning what I was seeing, I investigated it. I was always drawn to and intrigued by mysteries, so I decided to follow my intuition and see where it would lead me.

At this time of my life, I had been practicing my online readings and getting to know my pattern and my own personal style.

I had been growing my spiritual gifts for about 6 years, learning with spirits. Then, in the fall of 2019 my guides came and introduced themselves to me. What I didn't understand was why there were these two handsome guys coming to me. What were they looking for? I felt at this time that this was part of my purpose, so I knew I had better continue to hear them out. The ride they have been taking me on since is, again, a *wild one!* Nothing could have prepared me more for what I was about to experience in the next years of my life and longer – literally! This will go on for the rest of my life.

I have been working with my boys for four years now as I am writing this book and I have loved every minute of it. Everything I have learned from then on was from Jim and Steve. They are the most loving, patient, caring, understanding souls I have ever met, other than my past loved ones, of course.

I trust them, I feel 100% plus comfortable with them, and very safe and protected. It's a pleasure to be working with them and getting their stories out, along with the truth of many things after so much pain for so many years. When this book is done, they will have peace.

I am going to back up a little bit before I describe meeting the boys, so bear with me, as this is an extremely important part of my story.

Back in February 2018, I decided to go out of my comfort zone and start offering psychic parties. I offered what I called a practice party for free. I met some amazing people. I did all the readings and we – the host and myself – both felt it went well.

I stayed to visit with her after it ended. As we talked more we quickly became friends. I felt drawn to her home and her property. So, I walked around the house and the yard outside. But things felt off to me. I was receiving visions of all kinds, and the spirit told me to take pictures, so I did. After we wrapped things up, I left, and I felt someone with me. I thought, *Okay, let's see how this pans out.*

I felt a negative energy at my heels as I was walking to my car, which I felt was from an older male. He had a lot of negative, dark energy and I kept hearing an accent, a Polish accent with a hint of Boston in it. He was attached to that house. He wanted to scare me and/or warn me. It felt like it was *his* property. This whole area I was in felt odd and not very welcoming, very dark, despite how cute and cozy and warm the house was. It holds a lot of deep, dark, and disturbing secrets.

The boys came to me a year and a half later. Because I was going through some personal things during this time, I was glad to have some distractions to keep me busy. I thought. *Okay, I have a few things to solve. This will be interesting...* Little did I know what was in store for me.

So, to fast-forward again, I met these brothers, Jim and Steve, in the fall of 2019. I continue to write with them daily. I don't know who enjoys it more. I love the messages that come through from my past loved ones, Jim, Steve, and now Sweetpea. She was the spirit who had come home with me from that party.

Jim and Steve told me that they knew about that little girl. They had brought her through with them, with Jim on the left, Steve on the right, and Sweetpea in the middle, and I felt the protection they had for her. It also feels like they have been together in heaven for a long time.

When the trio comes through, they are always so close together that it seems that the boys treat her like the little sister they never had. They have a lot of love and respect for her, and she has a lot of love and respect for the boys. I could not understand the connection that they had at this time.

Well, I thought, *maybe I don't have two investigations to do, I have one as these brothers and this little girl have a connection and history of some sort and they want me to tell their story.* At this time, I still didn't know the personal lives of Jim and Steve when they were on this earth. But I was about to find out!

Since this little peanut has been with me, I couldn't help but get the feeling that I have known her for a much longer period. I felt we had a connection as well, but wasn't sure exactly what it was yet, as I was still learning about and progressing my gifts.

Then I remembered I was told I had to learn by experience, so I had to find out more.

When I was five, I knew and felt that this was not only a sweet age to be, but it was also when things started to happen for me spiritually. There were many reasons why I felt this way growing up, such as my fears, memories from places I had never been to, and more.

The thing that stood out a lot to me was why I feared small places, especially the backs of station wagons. Why did I fear blood and any intense physical pain, knives, guns, glass, dark places like basements, and why couldn't I stand being confined, locked up, or locked inside of anything? Growing up, I was not put in these situations, not even as a punishment, so it just didn't make sense, because these responses are usually taught or brought on upon by others as torture, which I had not experienced. So why would I be feeling this way?

Last year, the boys answered this question for me, as they felt it was time to tell me why I always felt this way. We were communicating by meditation one day, and they said, "You are ready for the answer." I told them, "Okay, lay it on me." So they did. They showed me a vision of me at five years old, which would be in 1973, in the kitchen with my mom. I started to feel trapped, confined, and very scared, and I started to see blood and a knife, and a little girl being put into a station wagon, after which she was tortured and killed.

I could see a dark basement with blood and words on the walls. It was a cold, icy feeling to me. I couldn't make out the words, but I can still see them, and I feel that as a young child of five years old, I must have blocked this out. This was a very disturbing and scary thing for a five-year-old to see and go through.

What I was seeing remotely at five years old was the murder of this sweet little girl who came home with me decades later, from the party that day in 2018.

This was my first encounter with Sweetpea that I recalled, even though I had one long ago, on that hot summer day in July of 1973.

This is why the connection was so strong with her. She chose me to be her anchor and voice, as well as the boys, to get her story out and heard and bring her peace and bring her home. She was just an innocent little girl that was minding her own business one day when she was *spontaneously* chosen by a disturbed young man who made the decision that *that* day was going to be her last day on earth.

This is why age five is so magnified for me. As I type this, I have massive chills and goosebumps, along with much sadness and disgust that such cold-hearted people could do this – with no remorse at all – and get away with it. People like Devin continue to hurt others to this day, 50 years later.

Again, if *teachers* and *law enforcement* had listened back then and done their job, things would be different today. But again, the power and wealth of some and the weakness of others took over and set up a perfect storm for many years to come. The patterns of working as a team or not working as a team can result in choices that are made or not made in the right way and will always result in more destruction and pain for innocent people all around.

We all have free will; we do have that choice. But Miss Karma and the Lord will *always* come back and have the last word. It's only a matter of time. And the time has come for this story to surface and receive justice for all that are involved and put an end to this *perfect storm* that has affected many, many innocent children as young as three years old to adolescents, young adults, and even middle-aged adults, both male and female, for many decades.

With having such an incredibly strong connection with Sweetpea for my entire life and never having met her in this life, I knew I had to keep investigating and find out who she was, where she came from, what her story was, and why she left this world so early. How could I not? I knew I *had* to do this. I *wanted* to do this, and I *needed* to do this for many, many reasons – not only for Sweetpea, but for Jim and Steve, and all their family members as well.

I found it very sweet and touching that when Jim and Steve came to me, they would now have Sweetpea with them. They were protecting her, staying with her, and comforting her when needed, helping her try to make sense of what happened to her, and apologizing, as she went through this when she was only seven years old.

People assume that when we die that's the end, but it really isn't. There is so much more to life and to the afterlife than we know. This is just one of the temporary stops that our souls go through. It's not only a stop with happiness, love, joy, and kindness. It's also filled with crimes such as theft, rape, human trafficking, and murder. Unfortunately, some of us must go through the bad in our lifetime to create that balance.

As I started to investigate who Sweetpea, Jim, and Steve were and where they came from when they were here on this earth, nothing could have prepared me for what I was about to find out. But what I do know is that the dead speak from beyond the grave, and heaven, and people need to know that there are no secrets. You can't run and hide from past choices and wrong doings. Miss Karma will always come, and the Lord will always have the last word. It's only a matter of time.

And for Sweetpea, Jim, and Steve, that time has come!

CHAPTER 11

HEARING FROM HEAVEN AND "MY BOYS"

As I mentioned earlier, I met Sweetpea in February of 2018 at a psychic party I did with my business Hearing from Heaven in Tolland, and I met the boys in November of 2019. I couldn't understand at that time why this sweet little girl and these two boys were in contact with me.

But I saw that they came to connect with me as a trio, and they soon told me why they were coming to me, so we started to get to work.

The boys stated numerous times that they needed to be heard, as they were not heard when they were here. Within a short time, they trusted me enough to start to tell me everything.

Sweetpea was with us. She didn't talk much, but I got the feeling she had a lot to say as well. So, I thought, *I have a lot of work to do.*

One night, the boys came to me, and they brought Sweetpea with them. I started to feel the pain and suffering they had been through. It didn't make sense to me yet, but I knew that in time it would.

I knew I couldn't ignore any of the pain, suffering, and sadness I was feeling. This was about to be part of my life. Now, I must get their stories out.

Why are they in so much pain? Why did they die at young ages? Why didn't anyone help them with their suffering? Why were they ignored? Why were they terrorized? Why were they abused and tortured? Why was Sweetpea younger than them? Why would a young child pass away due to murder?

There were way too many unanswered questions that needed answers for far too long. This is *not acceptable*. It's time to get the truth out and their side of the story heard.

This chapter is about how I started to receive messages from the boys and how we started to work as a team to get their long-unsolved case solved in the right manner and bring peace and justice to all involved.

Jim and Steve came to me for help. Sweetpea came to me for help. We will as a team get this story out that should have *never* gone this long without answers or justice.

The boys started sending me messages through psychic writing and visions. The writings were and are in the form of rhyming, songs, and drawings, but they are very direct. It was unique for sure, but I understand why, as Jim loved the poetry and music aspect of things when he was here – and still does.

I love to see them rock out, playing air guitar and air drums. It brings warmth to my heart. Steve also loves writing, and he does most of the drawings.

Oh, and the riddles they give me are hysterical. They have me dissect and figure them out. They are truly creative with ways of getting information across to me, because they are still teaching me about my intuition and myself, not to mention my need to have *patience*.

I did start to finally receive visions from Sweetpea. At first, they were very short and sweet. After I met the boys, they started to show me more about her, which Sweetpea had them convey, as she was very young when she died and didn't always have a way to share what she went through.

The visions started with showing me places I had never been to and people I had never seen before. As they began flowing in, I started to make many notes and fill many books of the writings of the clues they were giving me. As of February 18, 2018, my life was about to change...

Team Butterflies

Jim, Steve, and Sweetpea told me what they wanted: They wanted me to help them by telling their story to the world.

The hope is that the police will be able to solve the cases of the victims of this vicious, soulless serial killer and his cowards that help him, and give them the peace that they need and deserve. Whether or not that goal succeeds, these three souls want the story told. They have told me that even that much help from me will give them peace.

We are a team of butterflies, and I am determined to help them on their way to peace, as far as I am called to.

The teamwork of Team Butterflies began. There was no stopping now, even if I had wanted to. The information just started flowing in, 24 hours a day, 7 days a week, 365 days a year. It never stops for me.

I have been prepared with courage and strength from the boys, Sweetpea, and of course the Lord himself, but still I couldn't and can't believe what I was seeing, hearing, and feeling.

I will be sharing some disturbing visions, as this is part of their stories that needs to be told. It was extremely hard for me to take these visions in and watch, but I knew I had to do this, and I did and still do.

Their side of the truth is coming out, and justice will be served to the ones that were involved then, and are still involved now, as these actions are still taking place. Many innocent people are still getting killed and the murderers are walking free due to the inaction of local law enforcement.

Not only that, but there is too much action from monstrous, demented family members and teachers, and many others from the local communities and surrounding towns, who have had a hand in this for many years.

A lot of the people involved in all these years have passed away, but they are also speaking the truth along with Jim and Steve as they are wanting the truth out.

The fathers of Vito and Devin (two of the murderers), who are still alive today, want their sons to pay the price. They taught their sons to hurt people, but now they want them caught, as they have gone way too far, and this has gone way too long.

It's time for this *perfect storm* to come to an end.

CHAPTER 12

RECEIVING INFORMATION FROM THE SPIRIT WORLD

We all have our own views and opinions about what happens after we die. When we think of death, some believe that it is the end, but it is not. It's only the beginning of so much more.

There is a lot we do not know or want to know due to our ignorance and the fear of the unknown. Again, we need to let go of narrow-minded thinking and opt for open-mindedness, where there are more options and answers.

When we die and leave this world, there are choices as to where we will go, and we want to live the most beautiful, peaceful life we can on earth by doing all the right things for ourselves and others as we help them and enjoy everything that this world has to offer us too.

We are all here for a purpose. We all have a job to do, and as I keep saying, teamwork is what is needed to make this happen. When a team member refuses and strays and does not work with the others, things go awry, and many people get hurt on many different levels. It just keeps snowballing until it makes that perfect storm.

We do *not* need, or want, a perfect storm. We *need* to work together. I have seen heaven and I have seen hell and trust me when I say you *do not* want to see hell. It really takes a lot to get sent to hell, and your actions while you are alive really determine whether you will go there.

With my experiences as a human being walking this earth, and as a psychic and a medium, I have seen a lot. I have seen real creepy things, disturbing things, non-human entities – you name it. But there is absolutely nothing more disturbing and disgusting to me than the story the boys were about to tell me.

The boys and I had gotten to know each other well by this time. Trust is here, love is here, protection is here. The foundation has been made and laid out. As I progressed with my intuition and gifts, things started to make a whole lot of sense and move in the right direction.

This is how I started to receive the information that Jim and Steve needed me to know. Sweetpea loves to chime in as well with her own information, as much as she can. The way these three sweet souls get their messages through is just truly amazing.

Jim and Steve started off with happy times as young boys and brothers. They truly were 100% boys. They played rough and tough, they got dirty, they loved the water, they loved spending time with cousins, and they were sassy. Everything was **"EASY BREEZY"** as Steve would say.

But things changed as they got older and moved to Tolland, Connecticut. They never had a chance to get their dreams off the ground. Instead, they had to use their fight-or-flight instincts.

These sweet souls were taken way too soon under the thumb of *several* disturbed individuals who attacked them repeatedly for years until they both passed away at an early age and *not* by their choice.

They didn't deserve to be treated this way. While they were in this earthly realm, they developed a reputation that wasn't really theirs. What people thought about them was actually because of the actions of several other individuals.

The boys were physically and verbally abused, and threatened by many if they didn't contribute in the ways these other individuals wanted them to. They would be tormented, warned to keep their mouths shut, to never to speak of what they witnessed, and watched constantly.

They had to be careful and cautious every minute of their day, every day. They had to participate in things that broke their spirits in many unimaginable ways, for fear of their lives. They had to keep hidden secrets - heavy secrets that were too big for anyone to carry at such young ages.

The burden and overwhelming guilt and fear got to be too much. They never had a chance to portray their true selves. When they did try to talk and tell someone, such as the *local police department* and *teachers*, they refused to listen. Therefore, their horrifying experiences continued to wreak more havoc on their lives and the lives of others, as they found more sadness, fear, guilt, pain, and distrust in their family, and with neighbors and the local police and teachers, local fire departments, and town officials. *Are you seeing the pattern of that yet?*

The reality is that, after we die, we do go to heaven or hell, and these boys went to heaven, where they are again with their family members.

We don't ever go away; our souls just leave our physical bodies and go through a process to get settled into the place where we are sent. There are no secrets in heaven; everything is seen from there.

As for what the boys knew before and after passing, they decided that they would have the last word (other than the Lord, of course).

Jim and Steve will seek justice, peace, and freedom with the truth that has damaged their names, their minds, their hearts, and their lives with secrets that have been hidden for so many years.

I met Sweetpea in 2018 and the boys in 2019. At this time, I was getting messages, visions, and odd feelings that had begun that day in February 2018. That's the day that Sweetpea came home with me, and she has been with me ever since.

The visions I would see would make absolutely no sense to me at this time. I never forgot them and never will. Once the boys started to bring Sweetpea in with them when we connected, things kind of made sense. But all I knew at that point was that they were connected somehow, and I was the one they chose to sort it out.

The odd feelings I started to get came when I was driving. A vision would come, and I would sometimes have to pull over to process what I was seeing and focus on the information. This was happening a lot – and I mean a lot.

I would start to get information in our writings with words and names, telephone numbers, addresses of residences, and businesses in and around Tolland, Connecticut as well as places in other states, such as upstate New York; Bangor, New York; and Bangor, Maine.

The drawings and the rhyming/poetry would come next. I thought it was magnificent. The boys would want me to figure out the riddles (again, patience was needed, LOL). They would make me think and use my intuition and trust myself. Once I did, the messages just flowed right in 24/7/365.

No matter where I was, what I was doing, or who I was with, those messages came in. I would have to make notes right away.

What I thought was cool and truly incredible was when they gave me directions to literally go somewhere. They would give detail in feet, inches, yards, miles; whether it was day or nighttime; north, east, south, west, and tell me to see something or get something that had something to do with their story.

I started to make notes of what I was seeing in my dreams, and in those visions, I saw, heard, felt, and knew where I was and what was around me when these things happened.

I started to notice a pattern of where I was, and the connections that I had that were tied to this as well.

It's truly uncanny and surreal.

CHAPTER 13

GATHERING ALL
THE INFORMATION

The last eight years have been very long ones. So much has happened in my life, from my parents passing and family issues to figuring out where I stood with my intuition and psychic gifts and mediumship, and learning to understand and accept them while trying to get my business going and meeting Sweetpea and the boys. And then I had to figure out why they chose me and what they needed me to do.

After I found out who and what I was, I became very intrigued, and understood and accepted what was happening. This is my passion and the reason why I am here, to help others in any way I can, living or dead.

When I started to receive visions, they were very odd to me. They always came with a weird feeling. They never came in any order, and they seemed to skip around a lot. Some looked like an old movie on a projector reel, and when they came in like that, there was vivid detail. It was in many different eras, particularly the 1960s, 1970s, 1980s, and on until now.

I would also start to see words form and then sentences and see faces of people I didn't know. With some of those faces, I truly got the creeps, with an unsettled feeling and chills.

I would also have very vivid dreams with a lot of detail, and the same places and faces appeared in my dreams. Why? I had to pay attention to my dreams very closely. The writings and drawings they would produce came in detail, too. I just had to figure out what the drawings and the rhymes meant and where these things were located. I love mysteries and always have.

That was only the beginning. Jim and Steve would send me any information they could in any way they could, and when they started to show me different visions with the same names and faces of people, I knew something was very wrong.

But what I didn't know was that I was about to receive all the information for the next several years of my life and longer, on old and new cold case murders that were tied to Jim's, Steve's, and Sweetpea's lives and many others. They have chosen me to get this long overdue story out for all to have peace and freedom, except for those who are still alive and still committing these crimes. They need to pay.

I started to organize all my notes and began a timeline. I Googled the names, places, and businesses

I was told about. When I did that, I found that the boys were spot-on with their information. I took many pictures and videos where they would show me things as well, things I would never, ever have thought I would see in a picture or hear on a video. As a normal human being living a normal life, I never would have imagined I would be working on older and newer cold case murders and missing persons cases.

The boys were very good at how they would show me clues and lead me with real directions to the information that would help me when I was ready to go to the police. Everything was starting to make sense. There were and still are a lot of unanswered questions that have needed to be addressed for so many years.

These murders did not have to happen. They could have been prevented if only the local police had done their job. After all, they each took an oath to go above and beyond to help the public. But they didn't; some of them were involved in these murders, and others were too afraid of the ones who did the killings.

These police officers couldn't face off against the power and manipulation of these criminals, so they didn't keep to their promises as police officers. Therefore, there was no teamwork to protect the public. This failure resulted in many more brutal murders and crimes, which, again, continue to this day.

I contacted the Tolland Connecticut State Police with some of the information that I had from Sweetpea before I met the boys, and I did speak with a detective.

But she was less than interested in what I had to say; she was too busy flirting with another trooper to listen. She told me she would make a date and time for us to go over the things that I had. Then she ignored all my e-mails, and never returned my messages.

I spoke to the Connecticut State's Attorney in Vernon, Connecticut in 2018 and gave him brief information at the beginning of all this. He had someone take down all the information. A few months later, I went back to give him more detailed information and names. He literally ran and hid from me. He didn't want to talk about this, so he ran out of the building like a scared little child. Again, no teamwork, no justice. Just fear of these people and their money and power. This led to more murders and crimes. It's quite clear that no one in a position to help will help, so it's time to break on through to the other side and get it done. That's where the boys and Sweetpea come in.

Meanwhile, I continued to gather the information, as it was coming in fast. I have put it all together in books, including all the names I was getting along with the details of everyone's death, such as what they were wearing, the year, their age, where their bodies are, how they were killed, and by whom. They were all innocent people from the age of three up to a male in his fifties.

By this time, I had gathered information, with names and backgrounds, as to how over forty people were killed, and I have continued to get more names.

I have lost count, . There were and are so many more, and they have messages for their killers, and for the teacher who was involved, and for the local police who never acted on their promises. At this point, I am not sure who is more of a coward: the police, the teacher, the murderers, or the ones who have kept quiet all these years.

Over time, I have spoken to many, many police officers from surrounding towns in Hartford and Tolland counties. There was *no* interest whatsoever from any of them in hearing what I had to say. None of them would tell me where I could go or who I could give my information to or talk to about this.

These were cops whose ranks ranged from extremely high up in command to a regular cop on the beat. I have become so disgusted by how they just brush off people who have this kind of information, even when they say they are asking for help, just to cover themselves. They really do not want to be involved.

There was one police officer in particular who ranks very high up in the chain of command whom I asked for help. I asked him to please keep an open mind and hear me out and look at what I have. We played phone tag for four months. Then I got his answer: "Due to my religious beliefs," he said, "I don't like or believe in psychics. God doesn't like psychics. So, I can't help." I said, "God doesn't like murder either, and he does like psychics, as I work for the Lord." I asked if he could refer me to someone with an open mind and willing to listen. Again, the answer was *no*.

What I find odd, yet am thankful for, is that the murderers who have passed over since they committed these crimes – who therefore knew everything – are also now giving me information. They have chosen to help bring justice and peace to the innocent souls and put the ones still here on earth behind bars. They have led me to where there is evidence and shared many visions of what went on and is still going on.

I know that the police deal only in things that are fact-based and provable with the sort of evidence required for search warrants, but that's not the only way to go. That is narrow-minded thinking. They really need to be open-minded and hear what others have to say. Again, that is teamwork, and that is what will bring justice and peace for everyone, and get the criminals locked up where they need to be.

If this teamwork had happened, the people who they murdered would still be alive today.

Other people who are giving me information are the fathers and mothers of those killers that are still out there today. They want their sons to pay for what they did, and they will stop at nothing to make sure that they get what is coming to them. These fathers taught their sons to be evil and to hurt others, how to cover things up, how to lie and maneuver with tactics to the point that the public would never expect that they lived another life – a life of crime, passion, theft, working with the mob, jewel heists, human trafficking, and more.

One of these fathers was a local teacher at Rockville High School in Vernon, Connecticut. He certainly did an amazing job covering his tracks, until the last five years. This teacher worked with children, had children of his own, and even *adopted* one that he corrupted who is still committing these crimes. He is known as Vito, the boys' neighbor back then.

The other father had a family as well and had so much anger that he took out on his two younger sons. He taught one son how to lead a life of crime, he made deals with the mob and regretted it later, while the other sons, who we know as Jim and Steve, had to endure guilt, pain, and belittlement. He physically and verbally abused them until they couldn't cope anymore with what they'd endured, seen, heard, and were made to do, nor with the threats and other abuse heaped on them daily by their father and older brother. Suicide should never be an option. Or was it murder? I'm going with Jim and Steve's thoughts and what they have shared with me – *murder!*

These men and their sons have caused so much pain for so many people on so many levels, and no one will do anything about it to stop it. Their victims didn't want to die. Jim and Steve's father literally said to me, *"I'm sorry, I'm sorry, this should have never happened, I made a monster, and now he must be stopped."* He also told me he considered me as family and thanks me for helping his sons get this long overdue story out for the world to know.

Their victims had to die in cruel ways of all kinds, and all of them for no reason at all. Seriously, what could a three-year-old little girl, riding her red tricycle, having fun one day in the mid-1970s while visiting her family in Tolland near this teacher's home have done to make an adult kill her with a blow to her head and bury her in the basement of a home under the cement floor?!

What could a young woman in her thirties have done to her boyfriend, Devin, that was so bad he would kill her?! Did she know too much about what he was doing? Did she find all the trophies and other evidence he hid in his barn that he had from all his victims? Did she see him do something and question him? I would say yes, as he punched her face hard with his right hand, drugged her to make her drowsy enough to pass out, and then took her last breath by choking her.

Rose paid with her life by dating a man that she never really knew. When she found out what he was, he knew that couldn't risk her talking about it, so he killed her. He buried her under a large tree on his property in upstate New York so that he could keep an eye on the grave.

Little does he know that she is talking too, as she stands near her grave watching him and enjoying the birds that come to visit that area of the property where he buried her. R.I.P., sweet Rose. There will be justice for you as well. Making you go missing in the mid-1980s like you left town on your own, hasn't worked. You are a beautiful soul, and you will receive peace and freedom.

One of the facts here I thought was very disturbing is that the teacher was the mastermind of all this. He has made tunnels in his yard to bury the victims. He has graves all over the place inside a house, and outside that house, and in many other local places. There were so many odd things that made no sense at all when he was building this home. The only reason for them was to make it cover up all the evidence, bodies, jewel heists and all the unfathomable crimes that took place here on the property and in the house.

We don't need a teacher like that teaching our kids and using that role to commit crimes and to cover them up. He was a metal shop teacher, and he was quite talented. This served him later in hiding evidence. Now that he is speaking from the other side, along with his wife, the truth will come out. That's what I call teamwork!

Rockville High School, Rockville, Connecticut.

The mere fact that it was a teacher who induced so many murders and who inflicted such misery on so many people, and particularly children as they were prepped and transported to other destinations such as Mexico and South America from his home in Tolland, CT and another home not far from his. This is called *human trafficking*. These poor children endured so much pain going through this process. Good thing they had Esmeralda to feed and care for the kids before they left, because they didn't have an Esmeralda where they ended up.

To paraphrase Pink Floyd, these children didn't need thought control or dark sarcasm. They just wanted the teacher to leave all of them alone.

CHAPTER 14

"THE REAL STORY" TOLD BY THE ONES WHO WERE THERE

PART 1

The True Story

By now, I am hoping you are seeing the pattern of how this book is being laid out. I have explained and shared many things with you that I have endured in my personal psychic medium journey from age five until now. I know I have repeated myself a lot, but I had a reason for telling it this way. It needs to be repeated over and over to get someone to do something.

I have stated many times how important teamwork is in this world and how we should always help one another in any way we can. There is so much more I can share, but I will wait to put it in the next book as, again, there are many layers to this story. I think you get the gist of it. Kindness needs to be spread for so many reasons, it's the only way to live and move forward.

As I accepted these gifts and intuition from the Lord and became comfortable with them, it became clear to me what I am to do with them while I am on this earth. I need to help others in any way I can, shed light on things, open other people's eyes and minds, make them see the truth of what happened, and bring closure to others. My mission is to bring peace, clarity, guidance, and direction to others, without judgment, in a passionate, loving way.

I will continue to do this daily in my online chat readings, and in my personal life as well. I will also go above and beyond, go the extra mile too, to help the boys and, of course, Sweetpea get their stories out - stories that they have longed to have out for many decades.

In this chapter, I will tell the truth of what really happened to my Sweetpea on the day she went missing. I will share the visions and information I received from Jim, Steve, and Sweetpea herself *in detail* as they were all there when these things happened.

This will *not* be easy to do, but I must do this for many reasons, including bringing closure, peace, freedom, and justice to these sweet souls - and hopefully prison time to those who deserve it, as it's *never* too late to accept responsibility.

WARNING:

**Details May Be Disturbing
Reader Discretion is Advised**

The names of the individuals mentioned in this book have been changed. However, the names of the towns and places mentioned are all the real places where these incidents took place. The police have a hard copy of this book with the real names. My goal for this book is to bring forth the truth and action that Tolland County, Connecticut needs.

Please keep in mind as I write this it's extremely emotional for me as I had to live, feel, and watch everything that I am going to share with you, numerous times over the last five years. I will be as delicate as I can with the details, but the reality needs to be shared so that justice can be served after all these years. Fifty years, to be exact, for Sweetpea.

This will probably be the longest chapter in this book, because I want to put in as much detail as I can, as I/we see fit. This story is a part of me and my personal journey. There is no way I can't include it, as these cases need to be solved.

The families of the victims need closure and peace, as they have missed their loved ones for way too many years since they went missing with no explanation or clue.

Hopefully, this book will change that. This book will answer a lot of the unanswered questions for many. The *towns of Ellington, Vernon/Rockville, Coventry, Union, Stafford/Springs, and most of all Tolland, Connecticut, along with other towns and states will never be the same again!*

Please keep in mind that from this point on as I tell this story, I will be writing it with the visions as they were given to me by Jim and Steve, as they were present when this all happened.

July 26, 1973, was a hot, humid summer day in the town of Tolland, Connecticut.

Everyone was enjoying the beautiful summer day, going about their business. Sweetpea was a very smart, strong, vocal, independent, and sassy seven-year-old girl. She is telling me now that she was bossy, too. She enjoyed life as much as she could. She loved her family, and spending time with them was more than special to her.

On this one day, she wanted to venture out on her own for the first time after a day of shopping with her family. She was a confident, brave, and very happy child, and she loved butterflies.

She asked her mom if she could go by herself to get a butterfly that she had hidden down the road from her home . She wanted to ride her bike. It was a short distance, yet also a long one, as it was out of the line of sight of their home.

She pleaded with her mom, and finally her mom said, "Okay, you can go, but come right back," as it was late in the afternoon. Sweetpea was so happy and full of confidence that, for the first time, she was allowed to go out alone on this adventure.

As she got ready to make her first trip alone on her bike, there were other kids and young adults sharing the same joy that the beautiful day brought. There was a local 7-Eleven store down the road where a particular group of boys and young men often went to grab drinks and snacks.

On the way back, these men spotted Sweetpea at the rock where she was retrieving her butterfly. They decided to tease her and mess around with her for a bit. This was spontaneous. She was not targeted for *that day* – she was just at a convenient place at the right time to fall into the hands of these people. Her abduction was already planned for another day, but again Devin had the opportunity this day and he went with it. There will be more about this part in the next book. There were four people in this group, on foot and bikes, and Jim was one of them.

Sweetpea, very proud of herself, made it to the area where she had hidden the butterfly under a rock, but unfortunately, she never got the butterfly, and never made it back home again.

As she stopped on her sweet green bike with her feet on the ground, a young man known as Devin, the boys' older brother, started to tease her and call her names. She couldn't understand why he was doing this because she'd had other encounters with him, and he had been very nice to her.

He then pushed her, and pushed her again as she said, *"Don't push me!"* She fell off her bike, and hit the ground hard on her right side, which resulted in a torn ligament in her arm and a collarbone injury.

At that time, it was a dirt road, so it would kick up dust when it was traveled.

As she got up, she started to wipe the dirt off, and said, *"Don't hurt me anymore."* She was scared and crying and in pain from her injuries. She tried to get back on her bike.

Devin said, *"I won't, I promise,"* which he didn't mean. He became angrier, as he was going through some personal things himself. He was now full of rage.

Jim couldn't believe what he was seeing and hearing. He saw the eyes of the devil in Devin's eyes.

Devin had a drink that he had gotten from the 7-Eleven store on Merrow Road, just prior to meeting up with Sweetpea. He had the younger boys hold her as he put a pill in it that would make her lethargic and disoriented. It looked like a horse pill to me. It was big, and it was white, and then powdery as Devin crushed it. It was possibly PCP/angel dust, along with some type of downer.

Devin got his drugs from a doctor named Timothy Slotnic, who was also involved. You never knew what Devin gave his victims.

As the other boys held her, Devin forced the drink down her throat. Then they started to laugh and make fun of her again. She started to cry more as she tried to spit the drug-laced drink out.

Her eyes locked with Jim's numerous times. And then Jim took off, as he didn't want to see or hear anymore – not to mention the fact that he was scared out of his mind for his own life.

After the drug took hold, Sweetpea became disoriented. Her eyes were blurry and cloudy, voices sounded odd, and her limbs became weak. She could still hear and talk a bit, but it was hard to make out what was being said. She did hear the word *"Bangor."*

She just wanted to fall asleep, as she had no energy.

Decades later, 7-Eleven is a different business in the same building. One day, as I was driving by it, I started to feel dreamy, odd sensations, and there was a weird taste in my mouth.

I almost couldn't keep my eyes open. I had to really force my eyes to stay open so I could drive, because I could barely hold the steering wheel.

Once I got to where I was going, I pulled into a parking space and fell into a deep, seemingly sedated sleep for about forty minutes, and then I was myself again.

This is how Sweetpea felt after they gave her the drug in the drink. She wanted me to sense what she had experienced to get her point across.

Once Sweetpea was in this state, Devin and a few others proceeded to drag her sweet little body not too far from there, but it was a long and hot trip by foot.

Keep in mind that at that time, the area was all woods and dirt roads, and a lot of empty land with not many homes. But there were some. They were under construction then, and these houses would become the most disturbing homes in Tolland. They would hold many dark, hidden secrets beyond imagination.

Devin *forced* Jim and Steve to join them at the place where Sweetpea was taken, along with another young male who loved the Red Sox.

This fourth boy was wearing a Red Sox baseball cap, a Red Sox T-shirt, shorts, and sneakers. His name was Henry. He was younger than Jim by a few years, which would make him under 16 years old. He was also on the handicapped side of things, as they called it then, maybe mentally slow, or he had another disability of some sort. That young boy would be given a chance to grow up and experience life –until he passed away from an overdose later on – was it really an overdose? Suicide? Or murder?

They all arrived at *"THE SPOT,"* which is what I call it, and when I say arrived, I mean they were *forced to be there by Devin*. They did *not* want to be there. Jim and Steve knew what was coming and wanted no part of it.

They knew the pattern of behavior of their older brother, and that his actions would become aggressive, with a demented fire in his eyes, as he went into a demolition mode. But they feared for their own lives at this point, as they had many times, and did not want to die, so they had to go to *the* spot and stay put until Devin was done.

They were all led to a certain part of the woods, where there is a stream/brook. There was a large tree branch or log that was lying on the ground under all the pine trees.

Sweetpea's head hit a rock as he put her limp, defeated body down. Her head was facing east, and her legs were facing towards the west.

She could hear all the rustling in the pine trees, and smell and feel the sweat from the heat and humidity of the day dripping from Devin and could feel the dirt fall onto her as he started to beat her face until a tooth chipped and fell out.

Devin enjoyed this so much that he started to laugh and kick her in her tiny little belly. He kneed her hard. That took her breath away. She was gasping and asking, *"Why me, why?!"* She pleaded with him to stop and let her go. She said, *"I don't want to be here."*

Sweetpea started to foam at the mouth as the drug settled in more, and she started to cough up blood. Alongside her was Devin, of course, with Steve about three feet behind him, then Jim further back behind Steve, with Henry behind Jim, watching as Devin started to abuse and terrorize her more.

Then Devin *ordered* Steve to kick her in the belly and to strike her face. As I'm typing this, Steve is saying, *"I was forced to do this. I never, ever wanted to hurt this sweet child."* He feared he would be next if he didn't do it.

After he obeyed those fiendish orders, Steve tried to stop his brother by pleading with him. *"STOP,*

STOP, STOP, you have gone too far, man." Steve was exhausted.

Things started to heat up and fast. As Steve tried to tell him to stop and Jim looked on, Devin continued to beat her, slap her, and kick her beyond belief. He then decided that wasn't enough, so he sexually assaulted her. Then, like a proud peacock, he took out a knife that flipped open.

He then started to tease her with the knife and dragged it along her face, her bright blond hair, her throat, down to her belly and legs. He cut himself badly with this knife, so he now has no pinky and a scar. I've called him No Pinky for the last five years.

Sweetpea tried to scream. She was crying. It was now the end for her. Devin slit her throat repeatedly, until she took her last breath.

The boys tried very hard to stop him, but he would not stop. On this day, he turned into a monster that wanted revenge from someone who had nothing to do with his personal issues but would be kidnapped soon if they had not run into her on this day.

As Sweetpea took her last breath, things became quiet.

Jim vomited.

All of them were in shock – all but No Pinky. He was more excited and more proud of his work and all that he had done. He kept Sweetpea's tooth as a trophy to look at later. No Pinky had the boys cover her body with brush and pine branches until they could transport her to her next location, which would become her grave.

I was told there was another bystander watching everything that was going on. He was standing further east, about 100 yards away. He was wearing white Reebok sneakers, and his name was Bryson.

This sweet little girl had only wanted to venture out on her own to fetch the butterfly she had hidden for herself. She did that for the very first time with full confidence. Yet little did she know she would *never* return home again and life as everyone knew it would never be the same.

What happened to that butterfly that she went to get? I will tell you who has it. Devin kept it as another trophy, because he was so proud of his work. Anyone who idolized Charles Manson and the devil himself would be, and he was.

Within the next few days, Devin decided they needed to move her to make sure she wasn't found, as there were many search parties looking all around for her. Funny how no one in the search parties found anything. Devin thought of burning her body, but decided against it as that would draw too much attention.

And she was never found. She was put in a red/maroon station wagon with wooden sides. It was an early 1970s model that had a broken right rear taillight. She was placed in the far back of it where the back door swung open. She was wrapped in a brown/off-white-and-tan plaid blanket with tassels and was covered in some type of plastic, and possibly a blue tarp, then placed in a four-foot metal box Devin had purchased two days prior from the local hardware store near the 7-Eleven along with three other metal boxes.

That station wagon was brought to *"THE SPOT"* where she took her last breath, where she was thrown into the car by another guy, who went by the name of Bubba. He then drove to an area that was very, very close to where she was to be buried.

Her grave was dug, and she was placed about six to eight feet down at a house that was already built and had people living in it. Her right shoulder and collarbone were injured and she was missing a shoe and a tooth. Her blue shoe has Devin's DNA on it.

Bubba hid her shoe in the house in a wall before she was fully buried under the heavy dirt, rocks, and some odd type of pebbles and soil with some sort of gritty substance.

Bubba was shown to me as a husky man. His shoes stood out to me as the boys were zooming in on them for me to see clearly. He looked as though he wore a mechanic's uniform. It was a grayish-greenish color and worn out, with a button-up, a long-sleeved shirt with the sleeves rolled up, pants to match, and a belt with a semi-large metal buckle on it.

Bubba also had the same pebbles and soil substance that went into the grave on his dark shoes;

they looked like mechanics shoes. He had it on his shoes before Sweetpea was buried. This man had dog tags hanging around his neck. I have pictures in the writings done with Jim and Steve that show what the shoes look like, to share with the police.

Bubba has a scar on the right side of his belly. He may have been stabbed, or it could have been from a surgery he had. He was also wearing a ring on his right hand.

Bubba has had a disturbing life as well. His brother Boyd and their family have many hidden secrets. They both contributed to many of the crimes and murders that took place back then. Even his own relatives disappeared.

Even though he had separate issues, Bubba, Devin, and a neighbor named Vito teamed up together, with others. They continued this journey of murdering people of all ages, along with many other crimes like jewelry heists, local bank robberies (a bank in Vernon, CT in 1978), working with the mob, and with that teacher from the local Rockville High School in Vernon/Rockville, Connecticut.

There is no rhyme or reason to any of these crimes. There are so many layers of this story to peel. Some are connected, some are not. The fact is these crimes were committed, and nothing has been done properly for over fifty years to fix this.

As I said before, the teacher was a shop teacher at this time. He used this occupation as a cover for his crimes. He also was highly respected around Tolland and surrounding towns. He was quite powerful and had money. He came from overseas to this country to have a better life. Little did people know what he was really like.

Even with his Polish accent, he could fool people, and he knew it. This man was another monster, and he made his adopted son Vito into a monster, then Vito made his son, Rupert, the same – *vicious!* The apple doesn't fall far from the tree.

This teacher was the mastermind, the true crime boss of this outfit. Once he learned of Sweetpea's murder, he ordered the others to dig the grave and place her there. I was shown a yellow excavator. They must have used it to dig, because there were houses being built on either side of the house where they buried her, and six to eight feet is a far way down by hand.

There were tunnels running throughout the property for bodies to be buried, with underground access to the house, and a shed on the property.

There was also another man at the scene when Sweetpea was buried. His name is Ronny. Ronny was another man in a uniform that was like Bubba's. He seemed to have shaky hands that he couldn't control, and a twitch as well. He may have been a mechanic, or maybe he ran the excavator – or both.

Both of those men have passed on since this happened. Bubba went to heaven on an agreement to speak the truth, so he has been communicating with me about a few cold case murders and jewel heists, and showing me the beautiful jewels in a small sack inside a cement wall. Bubba has a lot to say as he confesses to everything he has done.

This teacher *(his spirit)* was the one that tried to scare me and follow me home from the psychic party I had done in Tolland that day in February 2018, the same home where Sweetpea has been buried for years now, along with many others.

That is the same house where I took a picture and she showed herself to me. Even though at that time this man was evil and had two sides to him, he is now talking, and he wants his adopted son, Vito, the creepy neighbor the boys talked about in previous chapters, to pay for what he has done.

This has gone on way too long, so he and his wife are a team *now*, as they both have passed on and are helping give me information to help the boys get this cold case solved, along with many others. *Are you seeing the pattern yet? Everyone wants this story out.*

Having the talent to work with metal would come in handy in such situations for hiding evidence of murders someone committed or was involved in. There was one metal box made by this man and or his son that was made to have a key to hide items in it and lock it.

Inside that box is evidence of Sweetpea's murder. In it, they put her *missing school papers*. I have the complete information and location of the person involved in that, and that will be revealed in the next book. There are also her little *blue shorts with a flag on them*, the *knife* with *Devin's and Vito's DNA* on it, and more. This box was buried in the same area where she was killed. It is wrapped in plastic to keep it from rusting and from the weather getting to it.

This box has traveled over the years due to the weather and the many, many years of the trees growing and their roots expanding. This box is still entombed after all this time. It has just traveled to another spot. When people say, *"If only the trees could talk,"* I can tell you, *"They can and they do!"*

As I am typing this now, both Jim and Steve are on either side of me with their beers, cigars, and two cans of original Pringles, munching away. They are watching and reading everything I'm typing. I love this teamwork.

These boys need to be free and Sweetpea needs to come home. I will get them what they need, and for many others who have suffered at the hands of these men. If only the local police had listened then, or would listen now, and have open minds, and look at what I have! I have the missing puzzle piece they need.

This little girl never got to grow up or have a family of her own. She never got to experience what most people do in their lives. She never got to finish school, never got to go to a prom, drive a car, kiss a boy, or graduate and become the person she was supposed to be. She would have had an amazing life growing up alongside her sister and their parents.

Instead, her life was cut way too short by the hands of a local man who was corrupted by his father and other locals into hurting people and committing many other crimes. This man worshiped the devil daily and brought a lot of negative and unwanted energy to town. Tolland County is a very eerie, creepy town that holds a lot of dark secrets that go way too far back in time due to these people. The woods, the water, the culverts , the house, the wind, the trees, and all the innocent souls are all talking and telling the story and they will not stop until something is done. The home will be having severe foundation issues soon along with water issues to get its secrets out and heard. This home will NOT be ignored any longer. There will be no escaping once the home starts to speak louder.

The police who were involved and the ones who were too afraid to get involved -the teacher, the fathers, the neighbors, and others from other communities - need to take responsibility for their actions.

This sweet little innocent girl never made it home on that beautiful hot and humid day. Instead, the small bike ride became a nightmare that no one should ever have to live. She was seven years old. No one deserved what she and her family got that day.

There are too many unsolved cold cases, and the lack of teamwork in them is just as disturbing and unacceptable. Yes, things were different back then, including the laws, the technology or lack of, the whole way of living life as a family. I can understand that, but as time went by, people gave information, and it was ignored. Again, this is unacceptable.

So many people have died, by murder of all kinds, from stabbings, hangings, woodchippers, gunshot wounds, beatings, drownings, or a combination of these.

As I am typing this, I have been shown four more murders that Devin committed. He shot a young man in the back and jammed his face and head in the mud until he took his last breath. This was in mid-March 2023. These people need to be caught. As my boys witness such actions with disgust, guilt, fear, sadness, confusion, anger, and more, they will have the last word until these people meet the Lord himself – or is it the Devil they will meet?

As I was receiving all the information about Sweetpea, I heard Jim say in a video that I took, *"Sweetpea is ready,"* meaning she is ready to come home!

I tried to tell the detective at the time that I had a lot of information to share with her, but she again ignored my e-mails and phone calls.

There are a few other visions that my boys showed me, of others who are also involved in this, but in a different way. They showed me a male named Grayson, who is tall with a diamond/oval-shaped face. This man looks like he enjoys the outdoors, and he wears a flannel shirt a lot of the time. I believe he loves to hunt, snowmobile, and all those types of sports.

He is also from a very big family, and a businessman. He married into a very well-known family that goes back many generations within the farming industry in Tolland County.

The vision that tied him to this story was that he was somehow involved in selling the house where Sweetpea is buried. He was showing someone the home. He was asked many questions, as people do when they buy a home.

Grayson was avoiding the questions and had to excuse himself. When he did this, he went to a part of the basement, and he was shaking a lot and had tears in his eyes. There was a lot of angst, sadness, and guilt on his face and in his eyes. He couldn't and wouldn't answer their questions. After he pulled himself together, he continued to talk to the people the best he could so he could unload the house.

Grayson knew what happened at this house; he knew more than he wanted to know and had kept it a secret for many decades. He also knew the previous owners and was trying to help his friend Vito successfully sell this house. This man continued to live his life under a mask and the thumb of another, who had and has all the control and power once again.

He looks like he has had a very successful life with a large, loving family and many friends, as well as a successful business and a few homes. He is very well respected by everyone. Seeing these visions, I am *not* impressed with this *jellyfish*. I'm *disgusted. He is* a *spineless coward*. I know he is full of fear and guilt, and now it's eating at him as he gets older. He is in his 60s now, and this guilt can't be very good for the heart condition he now has.

So, after finding out these disturbing actions and keeping them a secret until they start eating away at him, what does he do? Does he do the right thing and go to the police with what he knows? And he knows a lot. *NO*, this man didn't do the right thing. Instead, he married into a well-known family and buried himself in a well-known church and used this as a cover so that no one would ever suspect him of knowing what he knows, along with many other church members of this same church.

The other vision I was shown of him is that he is a huge Red Sox fan and makes this really known at his business, with all the decorations he has all around. This man was shown to me as running out of his office building by a back door after a certain someone entered. Again, avoiding the obvious.

All these years, Grayson has decided to hide himself in well-known families in the towns of Ellington, Tolland, Stafford/Springs, and Union. *Yes, let's not forget Union*, CT.

Apostolic Christian Church in Ellington, Connecticut.

Grayson married into this local family of farmers and set up a nice little perfect life for himself. I hope he has enjoyed this fake life, as it will be coming to an end soon.

This man did wrong. He knew about the house and property where Sweetpea was and was aware of all the secrets it has, and yet he kept his mouth shut for years. This man has *no* spine or balls to do the right thing.

This church won't save him; only he can save himself and come clean with what he knows. Maybe the police will cut him a deal. Maybe not, but he needs to take responsibility for the actions either way.

What's scary about this man is that he is around family and friends, children, and the public. In my eyes, he shouldn't be around children. He should be in jail. He will not be able to hide behind this church any longer as this property where this church stands today is also starting to talk.

CHAPTER 15

"THE REAL STORY" TOLD BY THE ONES WHO WERE THERE
My Boys

PART 2

The Victims

Here in Part 2, I am going to share some other visions that I've received over the past five years of other innocent victims who were murdered by these vicious men. I will be adding more in the next book as I am still getting visions and information daily.

Again, to protect their privacy, I will not use the real names I was given by Steve and Jim. I will use numbers instead. The police have their real names.

WARNING:

Details May Be Disturbing
Reader Discretion is Advised

VICTIM 1

A little girl came to me with the boys, showing me that she was here visiting family.

She was from a place that started with a V.

When I asked if it was Vernon, Connecticut, she started to hide behind the boys in extreme terror and clench her fists.

When she came back out, she had a pink flower and hairpins in her golden blond hair.

She started to show me how she was squirming to get away; she couldn't speak due to her throat being crushed.

She is very cold, and naked from the waist down with a crushed pelvis and hips because of having been sexually assaulted.

This little girl is confused, scared, and timid.

Her soul wanders still, because she is buried under the cement floor in a basement of that house in Tolland.

This was November 1974.

She was three years old.

She needs peace and freedom.

VICTIM 2

A young girl in Vernon, Connecticut was walking home alone when a man approached her from the front and another man, on the bulkier side, came at her from behind, covering her mouth with his huge hand.

These men were Bubba and Devin.

They put her in a white van, hitting her head and leaving DNA in it.

They drove her to Tolland, to a house that was just being built.

They kept this young girl in the basement of this house.

She was chained to a basement/garage cement pole. She was able to sit in a folding chair and or lay on a dirty, thin mattress that already had many blood stains from prior victims.

She was tortured for many days.

She was raped and beaten beyond belief until they broke her neck, then shot her in the head.

They placed this sweet girl in a well next to Sweetpea.

This was November 1974.

She was 13 years old.

She needs peace and freedom.

VICTIM 3

When the boys and I first started psychic writing, they wrote a name I had never heard before.

After some time passed, this male came through asking for help and showed me what had happened to him.

He revealed that he worked or owned his own business of some sort, like a contractor business. He met up with Vito and made a shady deal that he could not complete.

Vito and Devin threw him down the basement stairs. He hit the cement wall at the bottom and lost a tooth.

They then proceeded to beat him over and over with a crowbar, which Vito still has today. It has this man's DNA on it.

This was kept as another trophy, and it is hanging in Vito's shed. There was sweat, blood, and spit all over the place, and this male showed me where some of his hair fragments and pieces of the hat/cap he was wearing can be found.

After the severe beating, they handed him a shovel to dig his own grave. He is inside a large black bag with duct tape and buried near or in a brook/stream. He shows me a pond as well. I get two different visions. I do feel he is in a personal pond on the left near a divot with a couple other victims.

This was August 2004, and he was 31 years old.

He needs peace and freedom.

VICTIM 4

There was a male that came to town to find work to support his family. He was a small, short Mexican man in overalls. He didn't speak English well. He wanted nothing but the best for his family.

This man borrowed money, but in the end, he was not keeping up with the payments, and could not pay this debt back on time.

He pleaded and promised to pay it back, but that wasn't good enough for the loan shark – Vito.

Vito beat this hard-working, honest man to death and buried him in his personal pond.

I'm not sure of the month or date.

Age unknown, but he looks to be in his 30s.

He needs peace and freedom.

VICTIM 5

There is another male buried with the Mexican male in this same pond, on the left side, at the bottom, near a divot.

This man had blond hair, and was wearing jeans and a red, short-sleeved shirt.

I'm not sure of the month or year.

He was in his mid-20s.

He needs peace and freedom.

VICTIM 6

This next young teen was a runaway. She had dark hair, lightly tanned skin, and a spaghetti-strap top on.

She came across Devin, who tricked her into his web with his sweet talk. She got into his car. It was a dark colored car. I'm not sure of the make or model.

He began to beat her in the face. She escaped from the car.

She picked up a rock and threw it at him to try to get away, but it didn't work.

He then hung her from a tree, and she began to kick her legs with all her might to fight back.

She was able to leave a scar on his right forearm.

After she took her last breath, he took her down and buried her underneath that same tree and placed a large rock or boulder over her to mark the spot.

I have a picture of her that I took where she showed herself to me with the rope.

This was the spring of 1973, right before Sweetpea was murdered.

She was about 16 years old.

She needs peace and freedom.

VICTIM 7

Another female teen was really, really scared and shaking when she appeared to me.

She had a long white top on.

They put a plastic bag over her head and lowered her body into the water with her legs crossed and tied.

I'm not sure of the month or year.

She is not far from victims four and five.

She was around 16 years of age.

She needs peace and freedom.

VICTIM 8

This young man also came to me to show me his story.

He worked as a ranch hand on a farm/ranch for Devin in upstate New York.

One day, while working on the ranch in the barn, he somehow came across a box full of trinkets that looked like items that belonged to young girls. What he saw was a house key, hairpins, keys, key chains, pins, coins, and a bullet with dried blood on it. The thing that stood out to this guy the most was a butterfly.

He asked Devin about what he had found.

Devin became enraged and took an axe to the man's right ankle. The man tried to ask about these things again, and Devin attacked him again with the axe, then killed him by putting his body through a woodchipper.

This was between 1989 and 1991.

He was in his 30s.

He needs peace and freedom.

VICTIM 9

Another sweet teenage girl came to me, showing me that she was so sad and distraught. She was shaking, and all wet.

Her hair was on the dirty-blond side in color and was wet and stringy with blood. She was wearing an off-white, long-sleeved turtleneck and bell-bottoms.

She showed me how she struggled with her killer and had a huge fight.

He attacked her repeatedly. She wasn't sure where she ended up – possibly in a local lake.

This was in the early 1970s, possibly 1972.

She was 15 or 16 years old.

She needs peace and freedom.

VICTIM 10

This next female had thick brown hair down to the middle of her back and bangs. She had a slender figure and freckles. She wore bell-bottoms and a floral top. She also had the most beautiful eyes, as they were two different colors, one green and one brown.

She ran into Devin, she fell for his lies, and she got into the white van of horror.

He drugged her with pills (again from Dr. Timothy Slotnic) in a drink like he had with Sweetpea, which made her feel the same effects.

He drowned her in a local lake, and her body is still there.

This was in the early 1970s, maybe between 1972 and 1974.

She was in her late teens or early 20s.

She needs peace and freedom.

VICTIM 11

Another male was stabbed repeatedly and sliced beyond recognition.

All I was shown with this one was that this murder had to be done quickly because there was time pressure involved.

They buried him in a local lake.

This was in the 1980s.

He was in his 20s.

He needs peace and freedom.

VICTIM 12

This next young lady was extremely shy, but she wanted to show me some of what had happened.

She had long hair; it looked to me like it was dirty blond in color.

The only thing she showed me was that she was shot in the chest and buried in a lake.

This was in the 1970s.

She was in her 30s.

She needs peace and freedom.

VICTIM 13

Another young girl came to me for help as well.

She had brown, curly hair, with a little red.

She had a round, white face with some crooked teeth.

She was all wet, scared, and confused.

This was in 1971.

She was around 23 years old.

She needs peace and freedom.

VICTIM 14

There was also another male who showed me a large stretch of rope, which looked like a boat rope, as it was laid in a circle on the ground.

Two men tied this male up, gagged him, weighed him down, and tossed him in the water very late at night, with no remorse.

I'm not sure of the year or month, or his age.

This man needs peace and freedom.

Maybe it's time to drain the local lakes in Ellington, Tolland, Stafford, and Coventry, and other surrounding towns, and face the truth after all these years and bring closure to these innocent precious souls and their families.

VICTIM 15

There is another young girl who came from a very troubled family that held many disturbing secrets.

She was wearing blue clothing.

She went missing one day. This sweet young girl left home one day after a mishap of some kind. She went south from her home.

Bubba called Devin to come get her in the white van. It was cold and starting to get dark, and I heard it was around 4:30 p.m.

Devin used his sweet talk of lies to get her into the white van of horror. She trusted him.

They drove to Route 83 in Ellington, and he took her to Tolland. Then he started to threaten her. Her danger instincts kicked in, but she didn't listen to them.

She continued to trust him. She didn't think he was serious. He was nice and helpful at first, then he became belligerent.

He raped her, and tortured her many times over like he did with his other victims. He beat her until she took her last breath.

He then wrapped this young girl in a large blue tarp. She is heavily secured in this trap.

She was buried in the front yard that is now a garden at the same house where Sweetpea is. She showed me blue flowers and a blue stone. Her head is facing roughly southeast, with her feet pointing to the northwest.

This was in 1971 and her age was 17.

She needs peace and freedom.

VICTIM 16

Another sweet soul came through for help. She goes a bit further back in time. She was a young girl with dark, smooth, soft hair and tanned skin. She was wearing an old-time cross-your-heart bra with a cross pinned to it. She had on green clothing, including a pleated skirt made of thick fabric that fell just above the knee.

She was in Henry Park in Vernon, Connecticut when Devin came along and snatched her up.

He brought her to a stream, and he choked her and drowned her in the cold water.

What is odd with this vision is that I see two different timelines. One is July 1968 and the other is December 1968.

I first met this sweet girl when I went to the Vernon Diner. She would sit with me and show me that she was wet and drowned. This would explain the heaviness of her skirt's fabric. She showed me that the day of her murder was a very cold one. This was the first encounter Steve saw with his brother Devin in action. Steve was scared to death of what he saw and even more scared when Devin placed this sweet young girl's lifeless body in the back seat of Devin's red truck next to Steve. Steve vomited over and over. He was never the same again.

She is buried with Victim 15 in the front garden.

This was in 1968.

She was 13 years old.

She needs peace and freedom.

VICTIM 17

Another young girl, possibly a runaway, showed me she was beaten and strangled.

She tried to fight and run away from Devin. She hurt her leg and hip as she fell running from her attacker . She staggered and wobbled as she ran as fast as she could, but she couldn't't quite make it.

He put her body in an old septic system at the same house that holds many dark secrets.

This was in the 1970s.

She was between the ages of 12 and 14.

She needs peace and freedom.

VICTIM 18

My boys showed me a young male who was skinny and lanky with brown hair. He had on a yellow shirt with an alligator on the left side. He wore dirty sneakers, jeans, and a blue baseball cap.

He helped at a local gas station in Tolland, located next to where Dunkin' Donuts is today. He worked for or helped a man named Philip.

This young boy was bullied repeatedly by Devin. My boys showed me two steps that lead to the back of the gas station where he was pushed and thrown down. Devin ended up taking the boy to another place, where he broke his legs and arms with a bat.

I could hear the bones cracking as this monster laughed and enjoyed what he was doing. Devin and/or Vito either has the bat for a trophy or it's buried with this young boy. He is not far from Sweetpea, as he is along the banks of a stream.

This was about 1980 to 1982.

He was between the ages of 10 and 16, but the age of 14 stands out to me.

He needs peace and freedom.

VICTIM 19

The next soul I came across was a male. He drove a tractor trailer truck. He was a big guy with a beard and brown hair.

He made a deal with Vito and was unable to complete it.

Vito said, "Okay, don't worry about it," and sent him north to upstate New York, to Devin.

This soul felt okay about this, because he thought the deal would be complete if he did another task for him instead of paying his debt.

He drove up north to the ranch and met Devin.

Devin then killed him, possibly with the woodchipper, and buried him in the back left of his land by a large tree near a round-shaped fence.

This was between 2005 and 2010.

He was in his 40s.

He needs peace and freedom.

VICTIM 20

Another young male showed himself when I was at my retail job.

He literally popped in, full figure. He startled me, but I tried to focus on what he needed from me.

He was drenched heavily in blood, and he was very disoriented and dizzy. He was missing a tooth and wearing Adidas sneakers.

He had been hit on the head repeatedly and then strangled.

This was between 1986 and 1988.

He was 12 years old.

He needs peace and freedom.

VICTIM 21

I received another vision of a young boy with short brown hair and brown eyes. He had a rectangular face with a lot of freckles. The freckles are what stood out the most.

I'm not sure of the month or year.

He was around 10 years of age.

He needs peace and freedom.

VICTIM 22

The next female that came to me was a free-spirited young girl. She talked about *"flower power"* a lot.

She had on a long, thin fabric skirt down to her ankles. She showed me yellow flowers.

They buried her after killing her.

This was in the 1970s.

She was about 17 years old.

She needs peace and freedom.

VICTIM 23

There was another male who worked at the same gas station next to Dunkin' Donuts. My boys showed him to me.

He was wearing a thick flannel long-sleeved shirt. He was a smoker.

He was killed – strangled – and placed in a blue tarp in the banks of a stream.

This was in the early 1980s, between 1980 and 1982.

He was in his 20s.

He needs peace and freedom.

VICTIM 24

Another victim was crushed. She had dark hair and drove a green Dodge Dart.

This was in 1973.
She was 17 years old.
She needs peace and freedom.

VICTIM 25

This next young girl came to me in my dreams. She was very quiet and emotionless.

She was a black female. She was wearing purple clothes with some black. The fabric was a rough or bumpy silky kind. Her hair was short, soft, brown, and wavy with some blond mixed in, and the length was above her shoulders. She was on the shorter side, and heavyset.

No year or month or age.
She needs peace and freedom too.

VICTIM 26

This next young man was a slender white male. He was a country boy, dressed in jeans and a small faded checkered shirt. He was tall, with blond hair.

Devin buried him on his land near Rose, and the birds visit him as well.

This was between 2010 and 2017. 2015 stands out.
Unknown age.
He needs peace and freedom.

VICTIM 27

This next young man was different.

The boys told me he was a friend of theirs and an accomplice to Devin and Vito. He was tall and slender.

He worked with Devin and Vito. There was a brutal fight between these three. They ended up killing him and burying him in a "special spot" *for a special reason.*

When this young man came to me with my boys, he sat at my kitchen table, and he started by saying the following: "*Baron, Bates, Bobby, Robert. Irish descent, probable cause, not heavyset, 5'11", crabapple tree.*" Then he mentioned that his murderer's name is Devin.

This was between 1976 and 1978.

He was between the ages of 26 and 28.

He needs peace and freedom.

VICTIMS 28 and 29

The next two young people I got information on are possibly related. They may be brother and sister, maybe twins or cousins.

They were murdered and hidden in the teacher's house. The young boy slipped down after his body was placed in a kitchen island. The young girl was placed there as well, then moved outside to somewhere along the back of the home. She has bloody hair. The boy is wrapped in a blue rug that has two other people's DNA on it.

This was in the early to mid-1980s.

Their ages were between 12 and 14.

They need peace and freedom.

VICTIM 30

There was one victim that really hit the boys hard, even though they were gone themselves at this time.

It was their mother, Selena.

Selena was the second wife of the boys' father, and the stepmother of Devin.

This sweet woman tried to keep to herself. She didn't like to go outside much, but when she did, she didn't go in the sun or far from the house.

She had to live with fear, anguish, guilt, sadness, anger, embarrassment, shame, and so much psychological torture while being threatened daily,

On one day in January 1999, eleven months after Steve had passed, she was outside when suddenly she was struck in the head from behind. She didn't know what hit her.

The way I am seeing her death looks like a sudden shock, then nothing. She was out of her body very quickly.

She loved sitting outside (just not in the direct sun). She was found by Devin. Imagine that!

When they buried this sweet woman, Steve's ashes were put in her casket with her, and they were buried next to Jim. The love between the three of them will never be broken.

The boys show me a rose a lot when they talk about their mom. They say that their mom loved roses.

Now she will never, ever go without roses again.

She was 74 years old.

She needs peace and freedom.

VICTIM 31

The last victim I will mention is a woman named Paige. Paige was very sweet, and petite with her hair tied back in a ponytail just above her shoulders. She was pretty, with a slender body, and energetic.

This poor woman was shown to me in two different outfits. One was a small black top with orange pants. The other was a red dress.

One day, Devin decided to take this innocent woman to a field. He started to punch her face to the point that her teeth became loose, and her mouth and jaw were severely damaged and painful.

After he beat her face unrecognizably, she sat in the field crying and choking on her tears and blood.

This monster then watched her suffer a bit longer as he smiled and laughed. He enjoyed every minute of it. Then he decided to shoot her dead.

This sweet woman was Devin's flesh and blood.

She had given him life.

She was his mother.

She is now talking as well. She wants this story out and will help the boys anyway she can.

She needs peace and freedom.

I have spent the last 5 years enduring all these visions and feelings, knowing things and hearing the cries of these unnecessary, cruel crimes of all kinds happening to so many people for absolutely no reason whatsoever. There are so many more victims that I have been shown.

I also want to mention that I lived briefly for a few months in the home where Sweetpea is buried. I endured many unexplainable things in this home. The previous owner keeps an eye on this home, and when the homeowner rents the top apartment out, he investigates who is renting.

When he found out that I was living there and that I was a psychic medium, he began to step things up a bit, from breaking into the home through the basement to breaking the locks to my apartment three times. He also thought about putting a tracking device on my car but changed his mind.

He would keep in contact with Devin and the neighbors and have them watch me to see what I was doing and what information I might have access to.

I left after a few months, as it got too uncomfortable for the homeowner and her family. When I left, nothing else happened. It was quiet again.

For the last five years, I have spent countless hours, days, and nights working on this physically, mentally, and spiritually, along with the information I received from Jim and Steve. With their writings, videos, audios, and pictures, they know I have what it takes to break this open, and that I have the missing puzzle pieces that will do that. The police just need to listen to me.

I will make sure that Jim, Steve, and my Sweetpea, and even more innocent victims receive freedom and peace after all these years, along with their families. This story has so many layers to it, and it will surface.

This story will shock Tolland County, Connecticut when it finds out who has been involved in these crimes since the beginning. There will be another book with so much more information regarding the next layers that are unfolding now. This is for you, my boys, and Sweetpea. Your stories will be told and heard, and justice will be served. Always remember that what goes around comes around, and Miss Karma will always arrive at the door of those that have done wrong.

The grief, torture, and pain those people have brought to so many others are more than disturbing. These beautiful souls and their families need answers, and they need them *now!* They have been waiting too long. As they prepare for their loved ones' milestone anniversaries and visit the memorials they made for them, they are robbed all over again as the pain, the guilt, and the fear worsens.

My goal in writing this book is to motivate the police to take notice and to act. I have so much information to give them, but they need to be willing to listen. This is where teamwork comes in. If things were done properly from the beginning, these innocent victims would have lived longer or even be alive today.

I will *not* stop. I will bulldoze ahead until this story is fully surfaced and heard, and justice is served.

CHAPTER 16

THE FINAL WORDS TO PEACE, FREEDOM, AND JUSTICE

This is the final chapter in this book. It will contain the last messages from Steve, Jim, and Sweetpea to these people. They have had to relive all the pain again and again. Their energy levels were extremely angry when I asked if they had any last messages for their older brother Devin or for Vito or Grayson. They had nothing other than tears – many tears.

It's very rare for these boys to go speechless, and when I saw them sitting there with their faces in their hands, it more than broke my heart. These were not just regular tears, they were different. This brought me to a whole new level of anger. I was beyond angry. I had to get up and take a walk. I do not want these boys to feel this way *ever*. I let it go for that time, as I understood their pain.

I respected their wishes. I knew deep down that they had some last words, just not consciously yet. What I find odd is that these two guys have such beautiful souls. Yes, they were hellraisers, the bad boys in town, and heavy partiers, as most people were back in the 1970s. They were also the most loving and caring people and touched a lot of lives with their affection. They caused issues growing up, as most boys do. But they also tried to live their lives the best they could as they were living under a microscope.

They were not perfect by any means, but they tried to *not* be a part of their brother's criminal acts. They hung on until they couldn't handle it anymore. Both beautiful souls died under the thumb of their demented, devil-worshipping brother, and as they tell the story, they were both murdered. It was *not* suicide.

They were so different from him – these boys had feelings.

Their brother never did and still doesn't, as he still commits these crimes. He is a broken, empty shell with no heart, guts, balls, or spine. He is a coward, along with Vito and Grayson, and many others that were involved.

When I asked Sweetpea if she had any messages for him and all who were involved in her murder on that hot, humid summer day of July 26, 1973 when all she wanted to do was ride her bike, retrieve a butterfly from under a rock where she'd hid it, and bring it home and enjoy the rest of her day with her family but that never happened.

She said she would like to tell Gimpy, as she calls Vito because he uses a cane due to right leg pain, and Bubba, and Devin that she forgives them, *but* she wants answers as to why all this happened, and she wants peace for everyone left behind.

It strikes me hard that a sweet seven-year-old girl who was murdered can say something this strong. She has more empathy in her than all these people put together. She will be at peace when this book comes out. The only other thing she asks is that I go get her and bring her home for a proper burial, as her sister sees fit.

When I asked again if the boys had any last messages for their brother, other than them getting into his head and Gimpy's (as Sweetpea calls him) and messing with them.

My boys have shown me their fantasies for those murderers, and I love seeing them struggling in the visions I was shown. In them, they have no idea as to what's going on when they start to feel disoriented and lost. They find themselves going to places and don't know why they are in that area and doing things with no idea as to why they are doing them. It is quite hilarious to see them get some payback and watch them flop around like fishes out of water.

Steve and Jim looked at each other as I asked again. Then they started to shine flashlights on their brother and Vito, as well as Grayson. Their message is about bringing what those men did to light. I heard: *"No more secrets." "We want the truth out." "No more secrets, just the truth."* I also heard: *"You do NOT deserve to* live." "You need to pay for your sins and pay them to the devil in hell, as you may not be welcomed with loving open arms in heaven."

A more personal message from Steve is the following:

You have always been a mean, destructive bully from a very young age, as far back as preschool/kindergarten age. You have always gotten what you wanted; you are a spoiled, entitled brat.

Just because you had the looks you thought you could get away with anything. But guess what? You will be found and caught, tried and [will] go to prison, if you don't die by suicide first, seeing as you are a coward. Vito may pass before as well, because his health is declining.

Grayson has heart issues that may finish him off once he hears what is coming next for him. You both made a massive mistake, both you and Vito. You assumed once that these innocent victims were buried, that was it. You thought you were free and clear.

You're not, you see; everyone and everything is talking and it's getting louder and louder and it can't be ignored any longer. The pictures, the videos, the woods, the streams, the coverts, the lakes, the houses, the properties, the barns, the birds, the breeze, the air, the weather, the trees – all of it is on our side to tell the truth. The home will no longer be able to ignore the humans that are ignoring the signs. The foundation will open and crumble to get the attention it has longed for and to get the truth out.

You can't run much longer. Jim and I would like to dedicate a song to you.

"Renegade" by Styx, specifically the part about how the hangman is comin down from the gallows and you don't have very long your time is running out. So do the right thing. CONFESS!

You are going to face the consequences of your crimes, either in this life and/or the next because you have killed a lot of beautiful people.

We also pass along this meme to you:

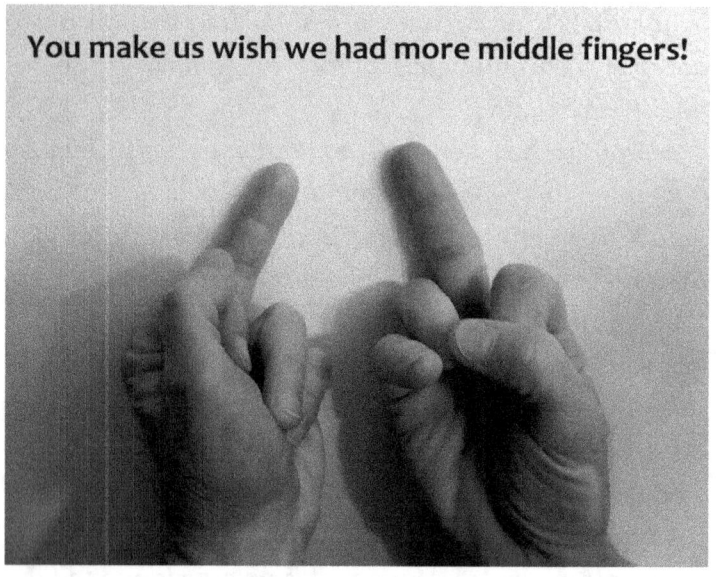

You make us wish we had more middle fingers!

This has been a very long and difficult journey. So many emotions, so many experiences, so many deaths, so much information, so many sleepless nights. I *never, ever* thought that being a psychic medium would ever be like this. I'm more than grateful to have met Steve, Jim, and Sweetpea, and that they chose me to be their voice and anchor to this earth to tell their stories for all the world to hear.

Jim, Steve, and Sweetpea had some final words for Devin and their notorious neighbor, Vito. Well, now I would like to say a few words to Vito and Devin. I am extremely disgusted with all the crimes you have committed. All the murders, from young children to adults in their 50s and 60s, to all the secrets that have been hidden for many decades along with causing so much pain for these victims and their families.

Your fathers taught you these crimes. Committing them gave you an adrenaline rush and a sick feeling of enjoyment and made each of you feel like a man. To be a man, each of you – Devin, Vito, and Grayson – need to start talking, tell what you did or know about these murders, and do the right things for the families of your victims.

The boys – *your brothers* – have given me so much detailed information now, these layers of this horrific story cannot be ignored any longer. The truth will come out when they find the four areas where you hid four makeshift boxes filled with many, many books with information on all your crimes, murders, jewelry heists, and bank robberies. Those books contain dates, names, places, plans showing the heists and robberies, mob information, border control information, and passports. These books were written by three people – the handwriting has three different scripts.

These makeshift boxes contain raw, uncut diamonds, unpolished gold and stones, bloody fabric, knives, guns, other weapons, and trinkets. The large brown book with a sun on it won't be hidden much longer, either. Let's not forget the large bank sack of cash as well that you failed to go back for and is now rotting in the river. That area has been investigated twice now, and hopefully will be a third time.

Vito was adopted by his father, and he learned to commit all these crimes from him as well. To show his appreciation, when his dad was sick and dying, Vito hurried up the process by killing him and leaving him with many bruises and broken bones, all out of revenge and greed.

This story has so many deep layers to it that the local police won't be able to handle it on their own. The FBI will need to be called in, because these crimes crossed state lines. Authorities from Canada and Mexico along with South America will be needed as human trafficking is involved and some of these crimes crossed national borders as well as taking place in the home of where the teacher had lived along with another house close by.

I know Devin feels defeated after all these years. I know Devin will confess to these crimes on his deathbed and will try to make amends. I for one will *never, ever* forgive him, Vito, or any of them for what they did.

I see the pain in my boys' faces as this book is ending. I see the fear, the anger, and the embarrassment; all of which they endured while they were still here. They still feel that pain. The times when I see them sad, angry, quiet, pacing, tight-fisted, crying, and moving to a whole other plane to process this again and get ready for this book to be released breaks my heart more than anyone can imagine. We all will have to do it again for the next book and possibly a third.

This angers me to a very high level that I just cannot describe. I want Devin and Vito to know that Jim and Steve literally *hate you* and they will have the last words, as will your very own dads, before you meet the Lord – or is it the Devil?! I hope all this was worth it to you – all this that enabled you all to live a lavish lifestyle, and to be well respected in town and surrounding towns, because it will now come to an end.

Again, this is about teamwork, and I hope this gets the attention of the State Police Troop C in Tolland, Connecticut. The hope of this is to get these cold cases solved and closed and bring peace to *all* of you who have suffered. The next book will have so much information in it, you just may want to confess now.

R.I.P. Jim and Steve

I love you both!

To the moon and back, and you know even further than that with me, as we have experienced a lot together.
Can't wait to see where we go next!

This is Jim, circled. His 1970s-style long hair is clearly visible:
His head is at 10 o'clock and his chin is at 4 o'clock.

This is Steve, above the arrow. He even has his mustache that he grew to cover up his scars of pain.

R.I.P. Sweetpea

Love you to the moon and back!
You can chase and retrieve
all the butterflies you want now!
You are at peace.
Now let's bring you home.

I will be donating 20% of the proceeds of this book to The American Foundation for Suicide Prevention in Connecticut in the real names of Steve and Jim. Even though they were murdered, they want others to know that they know what it was like to live with constant pain, emptiness, and fear. And to make it very clear that there is help.

ACKNOWLEDGMENTS

I would like to take this opportunity to offer my sincere gratitude to all the people who have helped and supported me through this, from the beginning of me learning my gifts and intuition to having my own business and believing in me and cheering me on to get this story and book out for the world to know the truth.

First and foremost, I would like to extend my gratitude to my guides, my boys Jim and Steve, and Sweetpea, for asking me to help them with their stories. Without them, of course, there wouldn't be a book. It has not been an easy task to make this happen, and fitting this into my daily life events, but I/we did it as a team. There is NOTHING I will NOT do for these three souls.

Second, I would like to extend my gratitude to my parents, who have helped immensely from heaven. There have been many meetings with them, and writings, telling me they are behind me with full support and extremely proud as well.

Third, I would like to thank my husband John, and our children Alice and Will, and a very special young lady that is like another daughter to me – she has helped a lot with this. Thank you, Kiera, for all your help and ideas and for keeping all this a secret until I was able to write this book.

Next, I would like to express many thanks to some wonderful ladies that have had my back more than once over the last five years. Stevie, you are my soul sister, my soul mate, and my sister and friend. I will always appreciate you and how you got me through the most devastating days of my life when I was at my lowest of lows, and you know how those are for us. I love you, sister.

Thank you for all you have done to make this happen, Judith, my psychic sis. You have comforted me and kept me sane during this part of my journey, there is no doubt about that. I will never forget what you have done for me, the boys, and Sweetpea.

I would also like to thank Leya Booth from *Reedsy* for re-editing and re-publishing this book for me. I appreciate everything you have done for me. Without you, this would not be re-published.

I would also like to thank everyone that knew I was working on this and gave their full opinion, whether it was your full support and understanding and patience, or your constructive criticism, which made me work harder to get this story and book out to the public. I'm glad you were part of this process with me.

ABOUT THE AUTHOR

Susan Sapolis Mahon is a psychic medium. She lives in Ellington, Connecticut with her husband John and their two children, and their dog, Dipper.

Her business is called **Hearing from Heaven L.L.C. – Psychic Medium Online Chat Readings** and can be found online on Facebook. You can also find her under the name Giftedmomma0911 on Keen.com.